CW00797736

BRITISH U
THE BREXIT MOMENT

Political, Economic and
Cultural Implications

Great Debates in Higher Education is a series of short, accessible books addressing key challenges to and issues in Higher Education, on a national and international level. These books are research informed but debate driven. They are intended to be relevant to a broad spectrum of researchers, students, and administrators in higher education, and are designed to help us unpick and assess the state of higher education systems, policies, and social and economic impacts.

Published title:

Teaching Excellence in Higher Education: Challenges, Changes and the Teaching Excellence Framework
Amanda French and Matt O'Leary

Forthcoming titles:

The Marketisation of English Higher Education: A Policy Analysis of a Risk-Based System
Colin McCaig

Cultural Journeys in Higher Education: Student Voices and Narratives
Jan Bamford and Lucy Pollard

Sexual Violence on Campus: Power-Conscious Approaches to Awareness, Prevention, and Response
Christina Linder

Higher Education, Access and Funding: The UK in International Perspective
Sheila Riddell, Sarah Minty, Elisabet Weedon, and Susan Whittaker

Refugees in Higher Education: Debate, Discourse and Practice
Jacqueline Stevenson and Sally Baker

Access to Success and Social Mobility through Higher Education: A Curate's Egg?
Stuart Billingham

BRITISH UNIVERSITIES IN THE BREXIT MOMENT

Political, Economic and Cultural Implications

BY

MIKE FINN
University of Exeter, UK

United Kingdom — North America — Japan
India — Malaysia — China

Emerald Group Publishing Limited
Howard House, Wagon Lane, Bingley BD16 1WA, UK

First edition 2018

Reprints and permission service
Contact: permissions@emeraldinsight.com

British Library Cataloguing in Publication Data
A catalogue record for this book is available from the British
Library

ISBN: 978-1-78743-743-2 (Print)
ISBN: 978-1-78743-742-5 (Online)
ISBN: 978-1-78743-752-4 (Epub)

ISOQAR certified
Management System,
awarded to Emerald
for adherence to
Environmental
standard
ISO 14001:2004.

Certificate Number 1985
ISO 14001

INVESTOR IN PEOPLE

For Ro

CONTENTS

PART III

CONCLUSIONS

LIST OF TABLES

LIST OF ABBREVIATIONS

BEIS: Department for Business, Energy & Industrial Strategy

ECJ: European Court of Justice

EEC: European Economic Community

ERC: European Research Council

ERDF: European Regional Development Fund

Euratom: European Atomic Energy Community

HEFCE: Higher Education Funding Council for England

HEPI: Higher Education Policy Institute

NSS: National Student Survey

REF: Research Excellence Framework

TEF: Teaching Excellence Framework

UKRI: UK Research and Innovation

VC: Vice-Chancellor

PREFACE AND ACKNOWLEDGEMENTS

A VIGNETTE: 'POLITICAL PROJECTS'

The point of departure for Britain's universities from their European Union-sponsored relationships with their partners on the Continent could perhaps be located in many places, most obviously Britain's referendum on EU membership held on 23 June 2016, which saw a narrow majority of the voting British public electing to Leave.

But the beginning of the long road to the Brexit crisis for Britain's universities might be traced back still further. In 2005, a Conservative MP named David Cameron had declared his intention to stand for the party leadership following the resignation of Michael Howard. Whilst largely unheard of by the general public, Cameron was a rising star in the Conservative Party, having served as a backbencher on the Home Affairs Select Committee following his election as MP for Witney in 2001. During this period, he penned a diary column in *The Guardian* newspaper. In 2003, he became both a shadow junior minister and vice-chairman of the Conservative Party. In 2005, he helped draft the party's manifesto as head of policy co-ordination. The campaign focused on fanning the flames of public anxiety about immigration, following the accession of the A8 countries in 2004, which was followed by a surge in immigration from those former Eastern Bloc nations. The party was accused of 'dog whistle' racism as a result. Following the defeat, Cameron became Shadow Education Secretary.

Cameron swiftly disavowed the manifesto and rebranded himself a 'liberal conservative' and a 'moderniser'. The 'Notting Hill' set which clustered around him followed New Labour's previous modernisation agenda with gusto (Finn M., 2015b, p. 35). Tony Blair had declaimed the centre ground as the place to fight and win in British politics; Cameron's agenda was to move the Conservative Party there after two successive general election campaigns where the party had run to the right, with dire results.

Cameron's background as a former PR consultant and his comparative mastery of public speaking and communications (when contrasted with his chief rival David Davis) saw him build a following. After the Conservative Party Conference in September 2005, he moved into the lead. In December, he was elected as Leader of the Conservative Party.

But that is not the whole story. Whereas Tony Blair in his 1994 campaign had sought to emphasise the legacy of his predecessor John Smith (Finn & Seldon, 2013), whilst making it clear his intention was to face down his party — as he did less than a year later over Clause IV — Cameron's journey was one of compromise. Despite three successive election defeats and a sense of crisis in Conservative politics, they had not sustained the psychological shock that Labour had in 1983 under Michael Foot; a 'never again' moment which gave grist to the mill of successive leaders — Kinnock, Smith, Blair — to remake the Labour Party in order to 'save' it.

Not all Conservatives, who in many cases regarded themselves as the 'natural' party of government, were as convinced that the party needed 'saving' in quite the same way. For some parliamentarians, Cameron was a scion of the gilded aristocracy who felt himself entitled to lead. For others, his newly trumpeted liberal Conservatism wasn't really Conservatism at all — and certainly not Conservatism of the Thatcher variety.

Cameron needed to give the right of the Conservative Party something. Something that would assuage their fears that he would change the party out of all recognition. Something that would remind them that he was, at the end of the day, a Tory.

Given that the previous two election campaigns had focused attention on Britain's relationship with Europe — in 2001 William Hague's *cri de coeur* to 'save the pound', and in 2005 the 'it's not racist to talk about immigration' approach which Cameron had been involved in developing — it was natural enough that Europe should remain central to the party's concerns. Cameron knew that he was perceived to be 'weak' on Europe when contrasted with his rival Davis, a figure with impeccable Eurosceptic credentials.

So, Cameron declared that, if elected leader, he would withdraw the party from the European People's Party (EPP), the main Conservative grouping in the European Parliament (Smith, The UK's Journeys Into and Out of the EU: Destinations Unknown, 2017, p. 59). The EPP was too feder-alist, too Europhilic. Britain needed to stand up to Europe, and the best way to do that was to build a new alliance with other like-minded parties.

The story of David Cameron's political life has a certain poetic quality to it. 'In my beginning is my end', T. S. Eliot wrote. This was nowhere truer than in Cameron's case. With the EPP decision, a decision of note only to political anoraks and those it was intended to hit home with — Conservative members — Cameron mortgaged the future of his leadership and any potential premiership to the goodwill of the

Eurosceptic Right. Subsequently, Cameron gained a (justified) reputation as an arrogant political gambler (Kettle, 2016). As Prime Minister, Cameron would later mortgage the future of his country — again on the question of Europe — to win a general election, promising a referendum on Britain's membership of the European Union if he were elected as Prime Minister of a majority Conservative administration (Smith, 2015).

Cameron was no true Eurosceptic, but as with successive British leaders, he was prepared to play that card when it suited him to appease his doubters, never imagining it would come back to haunt him. Even prior to the referendum, the EPP decision hit Cameron — and by extension, Britain — hard. Conservative MEPs' marginalisation in the European Parliament meant they had little say in the election of the new President of the European Commission in 2014. That was the first year that MEPs had been able to wield such influence. As Chris Bickerton describes, 'the main party groups ... nominate their "top candidate" for the presidency ... The candidate from the group that wins most seats gets the job' (Bickerton, 2016, p. 24).

The EPP won the most seats, and that meant their preferred candidate, Jean-Claude Juncker, would be president. But Britain's Conservatives no longer sat in the EPP, so they had had no say in the nomination. Cameron tried to frustrate Juncker's election, arguing that 'the authority to nominate the President of the European Commission lay with member states, not with the European Parliament. Cameron lost' (Bickerton, 2016, p. 24).

Cameron would then be compelled, as a result of a choice he had taken years previously for reasons of political calculation, to renegotiate Britain's relationship with the European Union ahead of his promised referendum with parties including a man he had publicly condemned and proclaimed as an adversary (Watt, 2014). For all the Eurosceptic cries that the Juncker nomination had been 'undemocratic', the truth was that it was the most democratic presidential appointment in the Commission's history, with the pan-European electorate of Europe able to choose their preferred candidate through the Parliamentary elections. Televised debates were held (Bickerton, 2016).

Why does this vignette matter? Not because it seeks to ascribe 'blame', or the totality of responsibility for British universities' plight in the Brexit moment exclusively to David Cameron. Far from it. Historians use vignettes as a literary flourish, because they are illustrative. Cameron's (mis)calculations in dealing with the EPP reflect Britain's relationship with Europe more generally — a more-or-less pragmatic engagement with the European Union for largely economic rather than ideological reasons. Britons — as a whole — never bought into the project of 'ever closer union'. In the 1960s, the British government sought membership of the then-European Economic Community because the Commonwealth was clearly not viable as a market. It was pragmatism that took Britain into Europe, even as a post-war, post-imperial political culture continued to trumpet British exceptionalism (Finn M., 2016b).

But Britain's universities — and universities within and without the European Union — did think of collaboration and the networks between them in more idealistic terms. British academics in the post-war period saw greater integration with their European counterparts as essential to forestalling the threat of war and, critically, the rise of demagoguery and totalitarianism within societies (see Chapter Three, this volume). Networks with European universities were long-standing, with strong Anglo-German collaborations in particular from the nineteenth century (Ellis & Kircheberger, 2014). In the 1930s and into the early stages of the war,

Britain had received her share of academic refugees from Germany and then occupied Europe. This helped frame academic views on collaboration and networks in the post-war period, with British academics (amongst others) playing a key role in the post-war reconstruction of the German universities they had once admired so much (Phillips, 1980).

Although Michael Polanyi might not have agreed with it, many in the scientific community across Europe saw its institutions as part of the realisation of a 'republic of science' (Polanyi, 1962) which transcended national divides. European subject associations flourished independently of the EU, but the freedom of movement guaranteed by the Union deepened and strengthened collaborations across the bloc.

In this sense, British universities have always been out-of-step with their politicians on the role of European institutions. To concede a point to those critical of academics' role in the EU referendum debate, this does indeed amount to a 'political project' (Hayes, 2016), though it is not clear to the present author why that should pose a problem. Universities have, at least since the later nineteenth century, increasingly seen themselves as international institutions with a global outlook, in sharp contradistinction at times from the nationalist politics which may flourish in their host countries. When universities themselves fall prey to such politics — either through assimilation as in the 1930s in Germany or through their potential destruction as in the case of the Central European University in today's Hungary (Economist, 2017) — these are taken to be the exceptions that prove the rule that universities are fundamentally international, and internationalist.

In Britain's case, that has also meant increasingly European. From the ERASMUS student and staff transfer scheme, to participation in Horizon 2020 and its predecessors, to collaboration with European partner institutions, to

Euratom — itself one of the founder institutions of the European project (Bickerton, 2016; Hinson, 2017, p. 4) — British and other European scholars, scientists and students have been drawn ever-closer together.

For the duration of Britain's membership of the European Union, Britain's universities were more enthusiastic about it than much of the general public, a divide brought into sharp focus when those universities were on the losing side in the referendum. As Britain's universities dust themselves down and contemplate their futures in tumultuous domestic and international political landscapes, this book seeks to highlight the prior character of the relationships they had — and have — with the European Union, with a clear agenda to helping those within them shape their own futures. In age of impact, where universities are consistently expected to be 'in step' with wider society, on the question of Europe Britain's universities have not been. It does not betray anything of what follows to note that this author thinks that this is no bad thing. But it does raise questions not merely about where Britain's universities go from here in terms of their international links, but also their place in wider British society — questions that go to the heart of what universities are for, and the agendas they can, and do serve.

This book could not have been completed without incurring a significant number of debts. Of course, none of those listed below are in any way responsible for the views expressed here, but they have each helped the author in their own way. Firstly, my thanks go to Kim Chadwick, education editor at Emerald Publishing, who both suggested the volume and then provided invaluable support throughout the process. In addition, I'd like to record my gratitude to an anonymous reviewer who made several suggestions for improvement. An enormous debt is owed to my research assistant, Hope Kilmurry, whose support was first-class throughout a necessarily-swift writing period. My former institution, the University of Warwick, was immensely supportive of me during my time as Deputy Head of the School for Cross-Faculty Studies (Liberal Arts) there, both financially through awarding me a grant to undertake work on Brexit and, yet more meaningfully, through the constant intellectual inspiration and collegial friendship given by colleagues. In particular, I should mention my friend, Gavin Schwartz-Leeper and my former head of department, Cathia Jenainati, for whom nothing was ever too much trouble. I would also like to thank my students who put up with a lot of chatter about Brexit throughout the 2016/17 academic year. They have suffered so future students don't have to!

One 'upside' of the Brexit moment and thus the writing of this book has been the collegiality of academic colleagues, many of whom I had never previously met. This include my interviewees — Professor Michael Arthur, Professor Stuart Croft, Professor Gerry McCormac, Professor Chris Husbands, Professor Simon Goldhill, Professor Robin Osborne, Professor Michael Dougan and Dr Rob Davidson all spoke to me on the record about substantive matters to do with Brexit over the past year. A significant number of academics and policymakers spoke to me off the record. I am grateful to them, and they know who they are. I am grateful too to Professor Mary Beard, who brought me into contact with the classicists, and Baroness O'Neill of Bengarve, who corresponded with me on issues of trust and expertise and allowed me early sight of her current work.

Old friends Steven Shakespeare, Gary Anderson and Lena Simic at the Institute of Advanced Futility were sources of wit, insight and enthusiasm in person and online. My friend Robin Brown discussed some of the themes here with me many times and the book undoubtedly benefited from these conversations. Tom Hunt of Newman University was kind enough to point me in the direction of some references. I should also like to note my thanks to Dr Craig Kelly and Dr John Firth for keeping me ticking over during this project and previous ones. Taking me away from Brexit during 2016/17 were my students, friends and colleagues at Liverpool University Royal Naval Unit. My thanks in particular to Captain David Morris RM, Chief Petty Officer Tony McTigue, Ms Julie Gardner, Lieutenant Anthony Gleave RNR and Sub-Lieutenant Annabelle Branch RNR for their friendship and senses of humour. Closer to home, my in-laws, Daphne and John, were generous hosts in the final stages of writing. My mother and father, Rita and Tom, endured more Brexit/unis chat than was either reasonable or healthy. Given the interminable minutiae of contemporary HE policy, it's probably just as well their love is unconditional.

Finally, my greatest debt is to my partner Rosie, who gives meaning to everything and to whom this work is dedicated.

CHAPTER ONE

INTRODUCTION: BRITISH UNIVERSITIES IN THE BREXIT MOMENT

*[W]e must emphasise the common element in civiliza-
tions, rather than the minor variations. We must teach
at all times the impersonality of knowledge and the
transcendence of values. We must dwell on the universal element in the human spirit. Above all, we should
set our forces against the intrusion into science and
learning of the anti-social forces of nationalism ... We
need — Britons, Frenchmen, Germans, all of us — to
return to the outlook and values of the Aufklarungzeit,
to that Enlightenment which stressed the unity of
humanity, rather than its differences. Without weaken-
ing the sense of duty to their local society, we must
seek to make our young men and women citizens of
that republic of mind which knows no frontiers.*

— Lord Robbins
'The University in the Modern World', an address to the
Conference of European Rectors and Vice-Chancellors,
Gottingen, 2nd September 1964 in *The University in the
Modern World* (1966b)

In this policy sector in which more is achieved by co-ordination and choice than by law, [the] EU has embodied the idea that institutions, individuals, and ultimately the state, become more competitive by being more cooperative. There is much that can be done and much diversity retained within systematised rules and values.

This notion is foreign to much of the British population.

— LSE Commission on the Future of Britain and Europe, *Higher Education and Research: Report of hearing held on 8 December 2015* (2015)

... academics have politicised higher education. The fact that the UK voted to leave the EU, against the advice of many academics and other so-called experts, has left many academics feeling depressed. Their political project appears to be over.

— Dennis Hayes (2016)

THE BREXIT 'MOMENT' AND BRITAIN'S UNIVERSITIES

Brexit and universities may at first seem disparate topics to a disinterested onlooker. One relates to existential questions about the place of Britain in the world, the other to the education of its people. And yet, even in that sentence, it is possible to discern — even before explicating economic links, political ambitions and cultural ties — how Brexit and the universities are interrelated. This is because the education of a country's citizens is never innocent of assumptions about that country's place in the world, and because universities — as institutions — at least to some extent, enshrine certain visions of the society they inhabit. Indeed, the sector-level analysis of an institution such as the university offers reflexive insights into the macro-level of the Brexit moment itself, since in many ways, Britain's universities and their relationships with the European Union throw into sharp relief the broader issues and problems the United Kingdom and its democracy must now confront.

Whilst much attention thus far has focused on how Brexit may negatively impact UK research funding (Finn M., 2016a; Engineering and Technology, 2016), or the security of non-UK EU staff (Savage M., 2017) or the appeal of UK universities to EU students (Morgan, 2017a) — and due attention to all these will be paid here — it's worth noting at the outset that this book is also an extended reflection on what the Brexit moment says about the place of British universities in the society they seek to critique, support and advance. This book then is a study of British universities in the Brexit moment — not simply Brexit's material impact on those universities, important though that will be in due course.

Its focus is on the implications of the Brexit moment for Britain's universities, and that word is carefully chosen. 'Impacts' would imply a definitive verdict. This book doesn't attempt that. What it does seek to do is highlight the potentialities of the Brexit moment for universities — in the hope that within this 'great debate' universities will be able to recover some measure of control over their own destinies. This book rests on the premise that we are living through a 'Brexit moment' in British political culture, of which the referendum itself is certainly the centrepiece, but which is not simply reducible to the referendum itself. The Brexit moment is the apotheosis of Britain's existential post-war dilemmas about its place in the world, but it is not merely that. It is a moment of profound interaction between those dilemmas and a genuine breakdown of the post-war British social contract, a breakdown in which universities are themselves implicated (in a number of ways). At the risk of oversimplification, this breakdown can be conceived of as follows: the 2008 financial crisis and the subsequent pursuit of 'austerity' policies by successive governments have resulted in a measurable decline in the standard of living (Butler, 2013; Hastings et al., 2013). Simultaneously, the gulf between the winners and losers of contemporary British political economy has become stark. As the Grenfell Tower tragedy showed so brutally, the gap between rich and poor in this country — the *real* value ascribed to human beings — costs lives (Eaton, 2017). The social divide in Britain has itself — in Baudrillardian vein — been commodified into the realm of the hyperreal (Baurdrillard, 1994). Working-class communities are demonised through reality TV shows from *The Jeremy Kyle Show* to *Geordie Shore*, whilst conspicuous consumption is celebrated via *Made in Chelsea* and *Meet the Russians*.

The popular perception that life-chances have diminished and the social contract has broken down has been growing. One interesting aspect of this is its generational flavour (Gardiner, 2016). The breakdown of the 'intergenerational contract' is a key feature of the Brexit moment (Gardiner, 2016). In 2010, Ed Howker and Shiv Malik published a book entitled *Jilted Generation: How Britain Has Bankrupted Its Youth* (Howker & Malik, 2010). In the book, Howker and Malik argued strenuously that the post-war generations had enjoyed benefits and life-chances out of proportion to their successors. As 'millennials' became demonised by their elders, often in the Brexit moment as a 'snowflake generation' (Fox, 2016), Howker and Malik chronicled the advantages the post-war state doled out to those same elders, from mortgage-interest relief to help them onto the housing ladder to final salary pension schemes and 'free' higher education after 1962 (Howker & Malik, 2010). The millennial generation, by contrast, entered the working world saddled by debt in a consumer economy driven by rising house prices and credit. The latter plunged them further into debt whilst the former made it increasingly unlikely they could enjoy the privilege of owning a home. And that is without raising the question of tuition fees, and the ever-growing cost of higher education.

At the same time, discourses of globalisation — integral to neoliberal political economy since the 1970s (Harvey, 2005) — promoted human capital theory as the magic ingredient in a successful 'knowledge economy'. This discourse fell on fertile ground in Britain, as we shall see later. Higher education expansion was the ideal vehicle for this vernacular human capital theory — more trained brains, more economic growth ran the argument. Though questioned by senior economists, notably Alison Wolf (2003), this has been the axiom at the heart of British higher education expansion over the past several decades (Brown & Carasso, 2013). Successive governments told the swelling ranks of students that the investment would be worth it; that a 'graduate premium' would subsist, making the fees and loans worthwhile (BBC News, 2004; Vasagar, 2010). The breakdown of this consensus in the Brexit moment, and the return of the tuition fees debate, is but a symptom of a broader socio-economic malaise (Sparrow, 2017). The comparative success of Jeremy Corbyn's Labour Party with the young in the 2017 General Election was at least in part attributable to 'his post-austerity platform, which included a signature commitment to abolishing university tuition fees' (Wheeler, 2017, p. 46). As the Vice-Chancellor of the University of Warwick, Stuart Croft, notes, for the young this resonated in the Brexit moment:

> I think the Brexit element is really important as well, as it's been interpreted — or it's being felt — I think

> by a lot of people who are student-age and recently-graduated that there's been a closing of doorways, a closing of opportunities, a closing-in really of everything … we've seen significant youth vote in favour of Remain, and even more significant votes in favour of Labour, who seem to be offering — quote unquote — 'hope' against some of the things around austerity, and around fees. (Croft, 2017)

But it was about more than that — it was about providing a 'credible alternative to the economic assumptions that have dominated British politics for nearly four decades' (Wheeler, 2017). Those assumptions — which had turned students into consumers — impacted across society and politics. The 2016 referendum result wasn't their Gotterdammerung, nor the 2017 election result for that matter. But it did mean that they were contested as they had not been for a generation or more.

The Brexit moment in British political culture — where the referendum is seen as a touchstone, rather than an isolated event — is the concatenation of a range of forces in British society, many of which universities have not been isolated from. One such force was anti-establishment sentiment, which reflected rising discontent with austerity, but which in some political guises also represented the outcome of the mainstreaming of far-right discourse (Stocker, 2017). Central to the Brexit moment has been the revitalisation of nationalism as a viable discourse at the heart of British political culture. Indeed, the very language of British higher education policy post-referendum has been emphatically nationalistic (see Chapter Three). A consistent feature of the referendum campaign was the prevalence of discourses on immigration and Europe that espoused a neonationalist frame for Britain and a 'dynamic reconstruction' of her historical memory (Trentmann, 1998, p. 230) in favour of nationalist conception of the past (and the future). This was a vision of Britain, and her place in the world, which was anti-pathetic to the 'networks' which characterised globalisation and its vision of global interconnectedness (Runciman, 2016a).

Yet universities exist within transnational networks, and since the medieval period always have done (de Ridder-Symoens, 1992). During the lifespan of the European Union and its predecessors, such networks have been facilitated, endorsed and even sponsored by the organisation itself. The revolt against networks, perceived by David Runciman amongst others, amounts to some extent to a revolt against the very values of the university in Western society (Runciman, 2016a). When the British public elected to leave the European Union, Britain's universities found themselves at one end of a gulf of understanding between them and a significant propor-tion of the population. As the Cambridge classicist Robin Osborne notes:

> One of the things that I suspect was true of almost
> everybody in the academic world was that it took
> the Brexit revolt to reveal how separate their world
> was and their set of expectations were from that of
> what turned out to be a narrow majority of the rest
> of the country. And I think no-one really realised
> that they were quite so out of touch. (Osborne,
> 2017)

Runciman enumerated university towns which were outliers in their region as Remain-voting bastions in otherwise Leave territory; 'Newcastle in the North East, Warwick in the West Midlands, Exeter in the South West, Norwich in East Anglia' (Runciman, 2016a, p. 5). 'University towns' were — according to the historian Peter Mandler — 'pockets of London-like entitlement scattered all over the country' (Mandler, 2016). For Mandler, academics contributing to the debate ostensibly on the Remain side exacerbated this gulf:

> The Remain campaign undoubtedly contributed to widening this divide. Rather like the *New York Times*' attitude to Trump, Remain thought it could laugh off Leave, or dazzle it with 'facts.' A very large part of the Remain campaign was focused on troupes of 'experts' — investment experts, science and university experts, fiscal policy experts — signing collective petitions and open letters declaring their loyalties to Europe. This played directly into anti-elitist sentiment. (Mandler, 2016)

Europe was seen as a good deal for 'the establishment', including 'experts' of the academic variety. Academics may not have seen themselves as part of the 'elite', but, as Osborne notes, this reflects their own distance from the wider public.

The implications for the university in Britain occasioned by the Brexit moment are profound. Economically, Britain's universities stand to suffer considerably because of Brexit. Culturally, Britain's universities have already sustained reputational damage as a consequence of the vote, but more than this have become more isolated from the national community they serve. Politically, British universities — fee-heavy, and unable to deliver on inflated government promises in terms of social mobility — stand in conflict with a government agenda aiming to repurpose them in the service of economic nationalism. These are but three examples of how the Brexit moment poses challenges to Britain's universities. As this book will explore, they are far from the only implications.

One theme, which has recurred consistently in the research and writing of this book, is that of citizenship. The historian Matthew Grant writes of 'three registers' of citizenship; that of legality, that of belonging and that of 'engagement' (Grant, 2016a, 2016b). In his 'first register', citizenship cuts across the topics discussed in this book in a range of ways. In 1992, the Maastricht Treaty developed the concept of European citizenship (European Commission, 2017a), which will soon be removed from British citizens post-Brexit. This removal will end their freedom of movement within the EU — and potentially more critically the continued possession of such citizenship will no longer guarantee EU27 citizens, including many academics, right of remain in the United Kingdom. But beyond that, it also touches on broader issues regarding changes in British state and society which were taking place long before Brexit. Labour came to office under Tony Blair in 1997 with one of their senior figures pledging to 'institute a modern view of the relationship between the citizen and the State' (Mandelson & Liddle, 1996, p. 192). New Labour — and governments since — became fond of referenda as mechanisms to gain greater legitimacy for decisions, or even abdicate responsibility for them (Flinders, 2009). This integration of direct democracy within a representative system posed fundamental challenges to the nature of that representative democracy, not least the place of expertise. As the legal scholar Michael Dougan puts it, in the Brexit context this has laid the groundwork for the regular democratic legitimacy of both Parliament and Government to be 'challenged by the irregular democratic authority of popular referendums' (Dougan, 2017a, p. 2). As the political scientist Matthew Flinders characterised it, by the end of the New Labour era Britain was in a state of 'democratic drift' (Flinders, 2009). This sets in contemporary context Grant's belief that ideas of citizenship in Britain are 'diffuse'

(Grant, 2016a). And this is without taking into account ideas of *academic* citizenship, which are customarily transnational and borderless. Meanwhile, in attempting to fulfil the requirements of Grant's third register — that of 'engaged' citizens (Grant, 2016a) — academics found themselves demonised. As Dougan puts it, academics 'who volunteered to perform the public service of participating in various debates surrounding the 2016 referendum' were met with 'ferocity' from some quarters (Dougan, Editor's introduction, 2017a, p. 5). This book then is also a study in what the Brexit moment means for competing notions of citizenship, and the problems which ensue when these cannot be reconciled with one another. Brexit may be seen as, at least in part, the failure to develop an authentic and successful 'European citizenship'. But this was not for the want of trying, and universities were — and are — at the heart of these conflicts in the Brexit moment.

THE BREXIT VOTE AND THE IMMEDIATE AFTERMATH

What is clear is that on 24 June 2016, academic citizens across the United Kingdom awoke to news the vast majority of them had dreaded: in the previous day's referendum, the people of Britain had voted to leave the European Union (Clarke, Goodwin, & Whiteley, 2017; Oliver, 2016; Shipman, 2016). At one academic conference taking place that day, proceedings were described as 'more of a wake … experienced academics, who thought themselves hardened to trauma by years of bombardment from REF, TEF and NSS, were almost in tears at the first session' (Edwards, 2016, p. 113). Within hours the Prime Minister tendered his resignation, and the United Kingdom as a whole was plunged into uncertainty, with the depreciation of the pound the first significant economic symptom (Allen, Treanor, & Goodley, 2016). At time of writing, for Britain, and her universities, that uncertainty still shows no sign of abating.

In the words of the new Prime Minister, Theresa May, Brexit meant Brexit, a meaningless phrase that could not hide the uncharted territory into which the United Kingdom, was now headed. Much of the pre-referendum debate had been conducted on two levels — an appeal to economics and an appeal to nationalism (Scott Crines, 2016); a dichotomy characteristic of Britain's interactions with the European Union over the course of their tortured relationship. In terms of the former, Brexit had implications for the whole of the UK economy, but nowhere was this truer than in the case of higher education.

Higher education has been a growth industry undergoing rapid expansion in the past several decades and is, by most indicators, a 'world leading' sector of the British economy. Looked at purely in financial terms, universities and other institutions of higher education are estimated to 'contribute £73bn' (at 2016 values) to the wider UK economy, 'including £11bn of export earnings' (Hubble, 2016, p. 3). Reputationally, the rankings which proliferate in the globalised higher education landscape routinely rate Britain's sector second only to that of the United States. 'Leading' British institutions (a phrase in commentary customarily referencing members of the Russell Group of research-intensive universities) typically feature in the upper echelons of the rankings, and in the past decade Oxford and Cambridge have taken turns at the summit of different league tables (Kershaw, 2011; Press Association, 2016). As Jo Johnson, the Universities' Minister, put it in a conference speech to university leaders in September 2016:

> Our universities consistently rank among the best in the world, with 34 institutions in the top 200, and more than twice that number in the top 800. UK

> universities are home to both world-class teaching
> and life-changing research, and they have been for
> many, many years. (Johnson, 2016a)

The dramatic expansion of higher education since the 1992
Further and Higher Education Act, which converted the former polytechnics into universities, and the concomitant rise
of the 'knowledge economy' discourse which promoted
higher education as both socially just and economically vital,
ensured that throughout the UK universities were — or
became — significant players in regional economies (N8
Regional Partnership, 2016). In Leave-voting Sheffield, the
city's two major universities — the Russell Group University
of Sheffield and the post-1992 Sheffield Hallam University —
joined forces to promote economic growth in the region
through a new 'prospectus for the Sheffield City Region'
(Morgan, 2017b, p. 36). A report in 2016 estimated that
eight northern research-intensive universities contributed
over twice the amount to the northern economy than the
income provided by Premier League football (University of
Sheffield, 2016). This placed the universities' collective contribution to the regional economy in the range of £6.6bn
gross value added (GVA), creating nearly 120,000 full-time
equivalent employment roles (University of Sheffield, 2016).
In recent years, universities have reshaped Britain's built
environment, with the construction of new buildings and
the attendant (and not uncontroversial) 'boom' in student
accommodation at the heart of towns and cities (Bennett,
2017). As Nick Hillman, the Director of the Higher
Education Policy Institute (HEPI), is wont to put it, when
searching for a university, 'look for the cranes' (Cocozza,
2017).

This shift in the economic 'presence' of Britain's universities was driven by a dynamic of expansion — in terms of

institutions and student numbers — which had characterised the post-war period but which accelerated dramatically after the 1990s. As Stefan Collini notes:

> In 1990 there were forty-six universities in the UK educating approximately 350,000 students. Twenty-six years later, following the founding of a whole raft of new universities, often based on an earlier college of higher education, there are now more than 140 universities with over two million students. (Collini, 2017, p. 1)

Brexit has economic implications for universities, to be sure. But it also has cultural and political ones. Universities are now more prominent in British public life and popular culture that at any previous point in history. A greater share of the UK population than at any previous point has an investment in them. Universities have gone, in Robert Stevens' phrase, from 'university to uni', from the margins of popular culture to the mainstream (Stevens, 2004). Once a staple of elite cultural forms, the image of the university conveyed in *Brideshead Revisited* has been displaced by the students of TV shows such as *Fresh Meat* and *Campus* (Finn M. T., 2012, p. 251). Universities are, as Collini recognises, constantly under discussion (Collini, 2017).

As we have seen, they were no bystanders in the Brexit drama, either. 'Nine out of ten university staff' were thought to have supported Britain remaining in the European Union (Morgan, 2016), and academics sought to use their expertise to contribute to the public debate (Dougan, Editor's introduction, 2017a), often on the Remain side. University-related interest groups proliferated, including Historians for Britain IN Europe, Scientists for EU, Universities UK and the National Union of Students (Clarke, Goodwin, & Whiteley,

2017, p. 14). The Leave campaign had its own academic interest groups and prominent spokespeople, but they were far fewer in number. The academic consensus was clearly for Remain.

But the vote's outcome seemed to imply that academics — and their universities — were on the wrong side of history. Less than two months before the referendum, the Political Studies Association (PSA) had published an expert survey which had claimed near-certainty for a Remain victory (Finn M., 2016c). This prediction was wrong, just as the PSA's earlier expert survey on the 2015 General Election had been wrong, and just as their subsequent expert survey on the 2017 General Election would also prove to be wrong (political science appears to have particular disciplinary challenges that transcend the broader issues around expertise; Fisher, Hanretty, & Jennings, 2017). Academics working in the social sciences seemed to be increasingly out of touch with popular opinion in the society they were studying, reinforcing perceptions of an 'ivory tower'-dwelling 'elite' amongst those who sought (for their own reasons) to do universities and their academics down. Yet academics' own opinions were in keeping with the much-discussed 'education gap' which defined the referendum outcome. Whilst nine-out-of-ten academics supported Remain, the likelihood of a Leave vote increased the less-educationally-qualified the voter. Whilst a clear majority of university graduates supported Remain — 57% — rising to 64% for those with a postgraduate qualification, those with no formal qualification saw a clear majority for Leave (Aschroft, 2016). Amongst the most likely to vote Remain amongst the whole population were those currently still in education (Aschroft, 2016).

Education was not the only axis on which the Remain/Leave divide fractured. Eric Kaufmann noted a split between those who subscribed to (broadly-speaking) libertarian/

authoritarian values. Leave support also correlated strongly with authoritarian values and support for the death penalty (Kaufmann, 2016). These are views not generally widely held on British university campuses. In terms of immigration, it is worth noting that even amongst Remainers there was also a significant proportion with concerns about scale. It was nonetheless the case that Remainers were more comfortable with immigration in general than their Leave counterparts (Morris J., 2016). This led to a number of more-or-less controversial analyses of the vote. David Goodhart, the longtime Eurosceptic proprietor of *Prospect* magazine, advocated a divide between 'Nowheres' and 'Somewheres'; this thesis argued in terms of what had become a familiar refrain in media coverage — that there really *was* a 'liberal elite' divorced from much of society (Goodhart, 2017). A small number of academic critics agreed. Dennis Hayes, an educationalist based at the University of Derby, characterised academic soul-searching over Brexit in the following terms:

> After the referendum, many … academics spent time publicly crying and ranting about the vote. Once the hysteria had passed, there was a period of agonising self-blame: 'We've failed as teachers!' 'What more could we have done?' But this lament wasn't about education, it wasn't about academics' failure to teach English, history, maths, physics and all the other disciplines that constitute the universities. No, these academics felt that they had failed to instil students with particular behaviours, beliefs and attitudes. There academics see higher education as having aims beyond the pursuit of knowledge within the disciplines. They believe that the university is ultimately concerned with 'social justice'.

> In other words, these academics have politicised
> higher education. The fact that the UK voted to
> leave the EU, against the advice of many academics
> and other so-called experts, has left many academics
> feeling depressed. Their political project appears to
> be over. (Hayes, 2016)

For Goodhart, the academics Hayes criticised would be part of a group he described as 'nowheres' — those comfortable with a globalised world and comfortable with transnational identities. 'Somewheres', by contrast', amounted to the bedrock of the Leave lobby — those uncomfortable with globalisation and its impacts, those to whom national identity was far more critical (Goodhart, 2017).

This diagnosis — though superficial — generated significant media coverage and built on the emergent narrative of a 'liberal metropolitan elite' which also drew on the more substantive contributions of Matthew Goodwin and Robert Ford on the behaviour of so-called 'left behind' voters in the years leading up to the referendum (Ford & Goodwin, 2014). 'Left behind' voters were by definition less educated and successful in terms of employment and earnings (Runciman, 2016b). This sometime-UKIP narrative — appropriated by significant Conservative Leave figures — existed in the same discursive space as Michael Gove's statement that 'we've had enough of experts' (Mance, 2016). The attack on expertise, and by extension universities, was a marked feature of the Brexit 'moment' and part of the reason it is best considered as a 'moment' in political culture rather than simply a one-off event divorced from wider history. It is one of the most significant cultural implications for Britain's universities posed by the Brexit moment.

THE INTERNATIONAL UNIVERSITY IN A DIVIDED NATION

Contemporary UK higher education is characterised both by its international outlook, and its international makeup. As one university leader, speaking before the referendum outcome, put it:

> Insularity is not the way forward, increased collaboration, sharing resources and ensuring mobility of expertise for the common good is the path we're on and the one we need to continue to follow. (Finn M., 2016a)

In terms of people, as Stefan Collini notes, 'overseas students constitute an ever-higher proportion of the student body (over a third in some institutions)' (Collini, 2017, p. 2). Students from EU27 countries amount to 5.6% of the student body in UK universities, or over 125,000 students (James, 2016, pp. 7–8; House of Commons Education Committee, 2017, p. 8). In 2016, there were 31,635 personnel from EU27 countries in the UK university workforce, equivalent to 16% of the entire staff in UK universities (House of Commons Education Committee, 2017, p. 13). This proportion is higher in certain fields and institutions (see Chapter Three). Around 16,000 British students annually spend some part of their studies abroad in the wider European Union as part of the ERASMUS+ transfer scheme (House of Commons Education Committee, 2017, p. 21).

Such internationalism is manifested both in financial terms and in wider academic links. Transnational research collaboration, often sponsored or promoted by the EU through its initiatives (including, but not limited to, Horizon 2020, the European Research Council (ERC), the European Research Area and staff exchange via Erasmus+), is a feature of contemporary UK academic life. This is not by accident. Whilst UK agendas in relation to research collaboration have often been driven by the political economy of globalisation and the relative strength of UK universities in a range of fields, other collaborations — such as ERASMUS — have had more deep-seated roots in the European project. As Cherry James notes, part of the rationale behind ERASMUS was the desire on the part of 'community politicians' to foster a 'European identity' (James, 2016, p. 16). In this sense Leave supporters and critics such as Hayes are right — the EU was a part of a clear academic-political project. But it is difficult to see why this is, in itself, a problem. Greater internationalism has been a *sina qua non* of intellectual life as it has developed in the West. As François-René Chateaubriand wrote in the eighteenth century:

> It will not only be commodities which travel, but also ideas which will have wings. When fiscal and commercial barriers will have been abolished between different states, as they have already been between the provinces of the same state; when different countries, in daily relations, tend towards the unity of peoples, how will you be able to revive the old mode of separation? (Rothschild, 1999, p. 106)

Prior to the referendum outcome few academic voices could be found to argue in the media that Brexit would result in a positive outcome for UK higher education. Academics from STEM (science, technology, engineering and mathematics) disciplines were particularly vociferous in the other direction. Scientists for EU, led by Dr Mike Galsworthy and Dr Rob Davidson, became a high-profile media presence arguing strenuously for the case for Britain to remain (Scientists for EU, 2017). Scientists for Britain by contrast, a Leave-supporting group, were fronted by Professor Angus Dalgleish, an oncologist and unsuccessful UKIP election candidate. But Dalgleish was notable by his comparative isolation (Tonkin, 2016).

Those who were more sanguine about British universities' prospects outside the union rested their case on a number of premises that subsequently turned out to be false. Some argued that fears — articulated by vice-chancellors and others — that Britain would be cut off from Horizon funding and wider European collaboration were simply scaremongering. Such scaremongering, it was argued, paid little attention to the reality that non-EU members were already participants in Horizon; Britain could expect the same (Wigram, 2016).

However, this analysis ignored an essential point. Such arrangements do not exist devoid of a broader political context. Many non-EU participants in EU research schemes do so on less favourable terms than the United Kingdom currently enjoys; none receive anything like the funding the United Kingdom currently does. In addition, the facility to access these schemes is predicated on contextual factors. For some nation-states research partnership is a step on the road to potential EU accession, for others participation comes as part of membership of the European Economic Area (EEA). The EEA gives access to the single market and many of the benefits of membership without the ability to play a key role in the EU's decision-making processes. In some cases — such as Switzerland's (House of Commons Education Committee, 2017, p. 20) — it also requires a commitment to the most contentious of the EU's 'four freedoms' in a British context: freedom of movement, which, with anxieties over immigration running high, was seen as a key reason why the British elected to leave the EU in the first place. Despite the 'Norway option' (and its Swiss cousin) being promoted Leave spokespeople prior to the referendum (Allegretti, 2017), with the arrival of the May government this option was ditched in favour of what became popularly known as 'hard Brexit'.

May elected instead to place restrictions on immigration as central to her Brexit positioning; this meant an unequivocal end to freedom of movement. This will severely impair the ability of UK higher education to function, as it places further constraints on staff mobility, but also actively disincentivises a favourable EU approach to British universities remaining in the European research funding framework. Those who argued that British institutions could expect a good deal from the Brexit settlement also failed to recognise that, important as UK universities are to the wider economy, they were but one sector. Some university leaders were shocked to learn following a Cabinet Office leak in February 2017 that education was considered by government to be a 'low-priority' sector which was unlikely to require as much support post-Brexit as others (Coates, 2017).

The challenges posed to the international university living in a divided nation transcend the economic sphere into the realms of the cultural and the political. As we have seen, one of the key characteristics of the Brexit vote was a stark educational divide between Remainers and Leavers. As we have seen, one of the strongest barometers of voting intention was level of education, with graduates breaking for Remain and those with fewer or no qualifications breaking for Leave. As Runciman has noted, this represents a broader cleavage in society in the era of mass higher education — between those with degrees and those without (Runciman, 2016b). An age-participation rate of 'close to 50% ... is enough to start splitting the population into two camps' (Runciman, 2016b). But whilst Runciman is quick to note that 'the education divide' is not simply 'another version of the [socio-economic] class divide' (Runciman, 2016b), it may be a cultural class divide of its own. Education has long been a significant 'form of capital' which in its 'embodied' state differentiates (in this case) graduates from non-graduates attitudinally (Bourdieu, 2002, p. 280). Naturally, this is truer still of academics. The proportion of graduates in the population is now so large that though they remain in a minority, the minority is so sizeable — especially in particular areas of the country — as to raise the spectre of what the historian David Cannadine describes as a 'dichotomous' mode of class representation; 'us and them' (Cannadine, 1998).

The growing awareness of 'the education gap' (Runciman, 2016b) in the Brexit moment begged a number of questions which prompted significant soul-searching on the part of academics and administrators in Britain's universities. This was particularly the case for those universities located in strongly Leave areas. The University of Warwick, to cite one example, is situated in south Coventry. Coventry — and the West Midlands as a whole — overwhelmingly voted to leave the European Union, a sentiment few of the university's academic staff or students sympathised with. And yet the gulf pointed up key issues — whilst international universities such as Warwick recruit students and staff globally, how integrated are they with their local communities?

Another tension was that of the 'impact' agenda. Nominally, the Brexit vote showed universities to be 'out of touch', and this fed into characterisations of the subsequently-demonised 'liberal metropolitan elite'. British universities, which now take as a unquestioned mantra the need to demonstrate the 'impact' of their research, took this to heart. Yet this book will ask if the Brexit vote reemphasises the need for critical distance on the part of the university, and examine the dangers inherent in being too responsive to trends in civil society. The impact agenda is a policy choice,

one borne out of constant reform in an rapidly evolving
policy landscape.

THE PREVAILING POLICY LANDSCAPE: BRITISH
HIGHER EDUCATION IN CONTEXT

The higher education policy landscape at the time of the referendum outcome was one of constant change, driven by
what Collini has described as 'market fundamentalism'
(Collini, 2017, p. 28). As Roger Brown has shown, since the
1980s British higher education — and English higher education most particularly — has been increasingly inflected with
the premises and language of marketisation (Brown, 2015,
p. 83; Brown & Carasso, 2013). It is worth noting at this
point that whilst the British marketisation process has parallels with the 'commercialisation' of higher education in the
United States and elsewhere (Bok, 2003), it is a singular
beast. British higher education had its own tradition of
reform and expansion in the post-war period which has
lacked an adequate history, and instead remains shrouded in
mythology. Two principal forces shaped higher education
expansion in Britain's post-war era; a liberal-idealist 'post-
war' conception of the university, which reached its apotheosis in the Robbins Report, and a technocratic advocacy of the
university as an antidote to geopolitical decline (Finn M. T.,
2012).

The post-war vision of the university as a liberal, critical,
disinterested, scholarly force has had enormous purchase on
academic self-perception to this day. It is an emphatically
post-war vision, articulated firmly at a time of expansion
from the 1940s on as a response to the spectre of totalitarianism as witnessed in Nazi Germany and as feared in Soviet
Russia (Finn M. T., 2012, pp. 48–96). This context (which

itself was never so simple) has been lost, but it was never true that the post-war British university was a simple child of 'welfarism'.

The technocratic impulse in turn is older than the marketisation literature, which focuses excessively on neoliberalism. Henry Giroux may well be right when he claims that neoliberalism has made 'war' on higher education, but the story in the United Kingdom is more complex (and ambiguous; Giroux, 2014). As historians such as David Edgerton have recognised, the university was perceived by policymakers in post-war Britain as a vehicle for arresting economic (and thence political) decline (Edgerton, 2005). This was true for policymakers of both parties. Indeed, at the outset of the New Jerusalem, debate took place at Cabinet-level about the extent to which universities could, or should, be bent to serve 'national needs' (Finn M. T., 2012, pp. 59–62). These needs, articulated powerfully by Herbert Morrison, Lord President of the Council and minister responsible for science in the Attlee Government, were conceived of in terms of a nascent human capital theory whereby Britain needed to make the most of its people in a world where she was no longer the dominant economic or political power. There was a deep concern within the state apparatus that universities lacked the willingness to respond to such needs, and advocates of scientific and technological education such as the twice Paymaster-General and Oxford physicist Lord Cherwell reached broad audiences in the 1950s (Fort, 2003). Higher education was discursively constructed in nationalist terms; the referents for debate were the supposed achievements of Soviet science (emblematised by Sputnik, which caused a transatlantic crisis of confidence) and the pre-eminence of US institutions such as the Massachusetts Institute of Technology. As Edgerton has shown, the 'two cultures' debate of the later 1950s and early 1960s represented an anxious Britain in truth not hostile to science, but desperate instead to maintain a role in world affairs (Edgerton, 2005, pp. 191–229).

As I have argued elsewhere, universities were never 'innocent' of the priorities of Edgerton's 'warfare state' (Finn M. T., 2012; Finn M., 2018a, 2018b). In the course of the post-war decades increasingly ambitious plans were proposed for alternative forms of higher education to alleviate Britain's perceived post-war malaise, from the foundation of the Colleges of Advanced Technology (CATs) following the 1956 *Technical Education* white paper (Ministry of Education, 1956), to the establishment of the polytechnic system after Tony Crosland's Woolwich speech of nine years later (Crosland, 1965). Even Harold Wilson's ambitions for the Open University, mythologised in Willy Russell's *Educating Rita*, owed something to Wilson's belief that Soviet correspondence colleges were giving the USSR an edge in the human capital arms race (Dorey, 2015, p. 242).

Many of these initiatives — the 'challenger' institutions of their day — were, then as now, intended to prod universities into action of their own. As Edgerton shows, the university did refocus its attentions on science (Edgerton, 2005, p. 3), but ministers and civil servants were not always happy with how university elites elected to reform. Under the chairmanship of Sir Walter Moberly in the 1940s the University Grants Committee (the predecessor of the Higher Education Funding Councils, albeit far more autonomous in terms of its policymaking function) sponsored the foundation of Keele University (then the University College of North Staffordshire; Finn M. T., 2012, pp. 97–116). As would become characteristic, academics subverted government agendas. Whilst the government-commissioned Barlow Report of 1946 (Barlow Committee, 1946) — which had triggered the Cabinet-level debate on universities — recommended 'at least one' new university (Barlow Committee, 1946, p. 17), the university which ultimately resulted had no material focus on science. Instead, Keele represented a liberal-idealist expression of 'education for a free society' with a multidisciplinary four-year curriculum anchored in a Foundation Year that did attempt to bridge the sciences and the humanities, but in truth was not geared towards producing scientists but 'active citizens' for a healthy democracy (Finn M. T., 2012, pp. 105, 114). In the 1950s and 1960s, the seven universities sponsored by Sir Keith Murray's UGC disproportionately took the humanities and social sciences — often with an area studies bent — as their focus (partly this was due to the simple fact that 'big science' was expensive; Finn M. T., 2012, p. 122; Sanderson, 2002). Finally, the Robbins Report — often (wrongly) seen as a document which inspired expansion which had in fact already been authorised — enshrined an ideal of higher education as a social good, driven by social wants rather than economic needs (Finn M. T., 2012, p. 248) Whilst publicly lauding Robbins, privately ministers and civil servants were frustrated that the famous economist had produced a document offering a philosophical argument for a particular kind of institution, rather than a determined attempt to link university expansion to manpower planning.

In 1964 Harold Wilson formed a government with a commitment to reforge Britain in the 'white heat' of the technological 'revolution', and the following year his then-Education Secretary Anthony Crosland inaugurated the polytechnic system with a broadside at the universities' purported intransigence and snobbery:

> ...we live in a highly competitive world in which the accent is more and more on professional and technical expertise. We shall not survive in this world if we in Britain alone down-grade the non-University professional and technical sector. No other country

in the Western world does so — consider the
Grandes Écoles in France, the Technische
Hochschule in Germany, Zurich, Leningrad Poly in
the Soviet Union. Why should we not aim at this
kind of development? At a vocationally oriented
non-University sector which is degree-giving and
with an appropriate amount of post-graduate work
with opportunities for learning comparable with
those of the Universities, and giving a first-class
professional training. Let us now move away from
our caste-ridden hierarchical obsession with
University status. (Crosland, 1965)

The opening of the 'great debate' on education by Jim
Callaghan as Prime Minister in the following decade, and the
rise of New Right discourses of marketisation due to the election of Margaret Thatcher as Conservative Party leader,
introduced new elements into the policy landscape (Ball S.,
2017, pp. 1–2). Whereas Crosland's vision for higher education for 'national needs' was anchored in state control and
the development of new institutions through a 'public sector'
of higher education, the post-Thatcherite vision was no-less-
directive but sought instead to resocialise universities through
introduction of market mechanisms and attacks on supposed-
producer interests. In the 1970s and 1980s the Institute of
Economic Affairs, a free-market, pro-Thatcher think-tank,
supported the foundation of the University of Buckingham,
the UK's first private-sector university (Tooley, 2001). In the
1988 Education Reform Act, academic tenure was removed
from UK universities, making UK academics vulnerable to
cycles of performance review and market pressures (Dnes &
Seaton, 1998). In 1989 the University Grants Committee, tra-
ditionally seen as a 'buffer' to protect university autonomy and
academic freedom, was 'abolished' (Shattock, 2012, p. 97).

In 1992 the polytechnics were admitted to university status and most began the process of academic drift which Crosland had anticipated in 1965, as Britain returned to a unitary system and (at least some of) its cultural values. During the 1990s the rise of the 'knowledge economy' discourse as a rhetorical vehicle of 'third way' politics, squaring the circle between what Michael Sanderson once characterised as 'social equity and industrial need' (Sanderson, 1991, p. 159), was embraced by both main political parties. As in the early 1960s, there was an arms race on whether Conservative government or Labour opposition could seem more credible in its claims to be most committed to education and the economy, nowhere more clearly enunciated than in Blair's infamous statement of his priorities: 'education, education, education' (Blair, 1996). For Blair, education reform *was* economic policy.

Senior figures in the Blair governments' education policy-making apparatus conceived of higher education as in need of reform, and in the later view of Blair's former head of policy, Andrew Adonis, academics as a 'producer interest' who were themselves an obstacle to such necessary change (Parr, 2017). Where neoliberalism was novel in British higher education was not in its diminution of academic autonomy, which had been a process sponsored by the state for some decades prior (and which would continue), but in terms of the shared discursive political economy which spanned both major political parties and which prioritised market mechanisms. Thus it was not a surprise that Labour reintroduced student payment of tuition fees in 1998, nor that it increased them in 2004 and commissioned a further review into them in 2009, which ultimately reported as the Browne Review under the Conservative-Liberal Democrat coalition (Brown & Carasso, Everything for Sale? The marketization of UK higher education, 2013). This was higher education conceived in terms of national economic necessity and individual economic return; market mechanisms, it was believed, could create equilibrium between the two in a way state direction could not, by fostering incentives to individuals to pursue subjects – particularly STEM – which accentuated employability and a high wage premium. This would, it was believed, have ever-more purchase as students transitioned into consumers and required a financial return on their (increasingly significant) investment.

Whilst post-war politicians eager to sponsor 'national needs' through higher education expansion had been careful to genuflect at the altar of academic autonomy and the cultural value of university education as a public good, by the time of the second Blair government such genuflection was notable by its absence. The Labour minister for higher education, Margaret Hodge, displayed a consumerist idea of citizenship (and a fundamental misunderstanding of the philosophy of taxation) when she condemned the idea that a 'dustman should subsidise … [a] doctor' (Finn M., 2002). Charles Clarke, the Secretary of State, meanwhile attacked medieval history as an 'ornamental' discipline in modern society, reinforcing the government's economic-utilitarian rhetoric on higher education, and legitimating increases in tuition fees (Woodward & Smithers, 2003).

By Gordon Brown's premiership, the proportion of students now attending UK higher education institutions had grown to the extent that the current financial system was no longer tenable. This prompted the review under Lord Browne, former chief executive of British Petroleum, which, reporting under the subsequent coalition government, recommended a lifting of the fee cap (Brown, 2015, p. 76). Though this was the most iconic moment of higher education reform since the reintroduction of tuition fees – narrativised as a Liberal Democrat betrayal of their voters – its true significance lay inasmuch in what followed. Successive universities' ministers in the coalition and subsequent Conservative governments sought to use market drivers to alter university structures and behaviour (Finn M., 2015c, pp. 88–89). With an emphasis on 'value for money' (VFM), the Conservative Party's 2015 manifesto advocated an increase in two-year degrees (already offered by Buckingham, and central to its core business model) and a fuller marketisation of the sector (Conservative Party, 2015, p. 35). The subsequent white paper promoted opportunities for market 'exit' for 'providers', completing the development of a market begun by the Browne Review (Department for Business, Innovation and Skills, 2016b, p. 10). Accompanying such change was the wholesale reform of UK research policy, by forming an overarching body to sponsor the subject-area Research Councils, named UK Research and Innovation (UKRI) which would be housed in the new Department for Business, Energy, Innovation and Skills (BEIS) (UKRI, 2017). The net result was a further deprioritisation of humanities and social sciences research in favour of STEM; the Nurse Review into research policy which pre-empted the formation of UKRI stated baldly that the head of UKRI should be a scientist of 'distinction', which begged the question whether candidates with humanities' backgrounds were even eligible for the appointment (Nurse, 2015, p. 27).

The Conservative government elected in 2015 also had as a manifesto commitment the introduction of a Teaching Excellence Framework (TEF) which would seek to reprioritise universities' attention towards teaching in light of the new student-consumer dynamic, and to increase the viability of the market through the provision of accurate information on the standard of education available at different providers (Conservative Party, 2015, p. 35). However, the TEF as realised did not measure teaching, but offered subjective judgements authorised by a panel based on proxies including university performance in student satisfaction surveys. That such surveys are open to gaming and reflect racial and gender prejudices amongst student populations (Deo, 2015) was ignored in favour of their use as the 'best available' data, thus encouraging further 'gaming'.

THE PLAN OF THE BOOK

In the Brexit moment then, Britain's universities stand in a state of permanent revolution. Even prior to the referendum vote, successive governments — since the end of the Second World War — have sought to motivate change within higher education in favour of perceived 'national needs'. These have consistently been envisaged in economic terms, and since the 1970s, in terms of markets. This is a key aspect of the contemporary British political economy of higher education. Yet, powerful as it is, it is not the only discursive 'frame' in which contemporary UK higher education is 'imagined'. The student protests and riots of 2010–2011 which centred on the government's decision to raise tuition fees paid testament to a residual 'moral economy' of 'free' higher education amongst the wider British public (Ibrahim, 2014). The same moral economy has been made visible in the aftermath of the 2017 UK General Election (Adonis, 2017). The Labour Party, having fought the election with a pledge to remove student tuition fees, found itself mired in controversy thereafter as to whether or not they had pledged also to reprieve existing student debt (they hadn't, though they had claimed that they would seek to ameliorate it; Roberts, 2017).

The persistence of this moral economy of higher education illustrates the rapidity of change in the UK sector. Though, as this account has noted, aims have been more-or-less consistent on the part of governments of different stripes, means have not been. In the 1960s, it was axiomatic for Labour governments that what was needed were different kinds of taxpayer-funded institutions, just as it was axiomatic in the 1990s for a subsequent Labour government that student payment of fees and an attendant marketised system were both necessary and inevitable. Yet the transition from 'free' higher education to £9000 fees took place so swiftly that the moral economy of higher education did not shift with it, and parents had no opportunity to undertake the decades-long planning that it is a feature of other marketised systems. This has led both to unpredictable consumer behaviour and a residual resentment against fees and the commodification of education which they represent, which transcends the supposed-producer interest and 'hyperbole' of academic critics (Hillman, 2016, p. 342). Into this clash of discourses came Brexit, arguably the biggest exogenous shock to Britain's polity since the Suez Crisis of 1956.

The Brexit moment presents an enormous series of challenges to Britain's universities. Many of their academics would no doubt feel they are ill-suited to meet them. A recent study has argued powerfully that the internalisation of the market-consumer model has been so complete on the part of university leaderships — with the attendant rise of a professionalised, non-academic, managerial class (Smyth, 2017) — that they are simply unable to deal with the unprecedented economic, political and cultural implications of the Brexit moment. Instead, such leaderships are 'zombies' (Smyth, 2017), slavishly adhering to a policy paradigm — neoliberalism — which is itself in a state of crisis, opposed from differing sides by the mainstreaming of neonationalist politics and on the other hand the return of a moral economy of higher education and anti-austerity sentiment anchored in non-consumer 'registers' (Grant, 2016a) of citizenship.

This book focuses on the three domains of these implications — the economic, the political, and the cultural, in terms of their relationship to staff and students (addressed in Chapter Two), research and funding (Chapter Three) and the broader place of the university in contemporary British society. The final chapter focuses on the political economy of higher education, to draw together these implications, and assess to what extent this has created a new political economy in the Brexit moment, and what opportunities are present for universities to reconstruct their destinies according to their own ambitions and values. To some extent, this book deals with essential questions of 'what are universities for?' though it does not propose an essentialist response. Beyond making a contribution to the study of universities in the United Kingdom, it also makes a small intervention in the broader Brexit debate, because the dilemmas facing Britain's universities — whist their own — nonetheless represent the practical manifestations of the wider political challenges facing the United Kingdom, not to mention the development of Britain's relationship with the EU into — and beyond — the Brexit moment.

PART I

———

THE IMPACT(S) OF BREXIT

CHAPTER TWO

STAFF AND STUDENTS

From a professional point of view, the mastery of English language and my adaptation to British culture have enabled me to seek a job in Great Britain and to get familiarised with the job market mechanisms, the interviews and so on. I hope to be recruited in some months, bearing in mind that the British market is more dynamic than the French.

— Anonymous French ERASMUS student, cited in Papatsiba (2005)

EU THIEVING STUDENTS: One in four European Union citizens who study in England go home without paying a PENNY of their student loans

— Headline, *The Sun newspaper*, 2 March 2017

The recruitment agency said it was quite scary, the number of applications they're now getting from EU professionals in the UK ... It's difficult to exaggerate how sad and angry and disappointed we feel ... We

*came here as teenagers, thanks to free movement.
We studied here, we met here, we've spent our
whole adult lives here. We'd never thought of
leaving. This was our home.*

— 'Alexandros', academic healthcare researcher,
cited in *The Guardian* (28 July 2017)

THE BACKGROUND: 'UNCERTAINTY' AND THREATS

The internationalisation — and Europeanisation — of
Britain's universities is most visibly represented in terms of its
staff and student bodies. Citizens of EU27 states make up
16% of staff in Britain's universities and around 5.6% of
students (House of Commons Education Committee, 2017,
p. 8). In the Russell Group of research-intensive universities,
these numbers rise — with 8% of undergraduate students
heralding from EU27 states and 21% of academic staff
(Russell Group, 2017). At individual institutions, the situation is even more critical — at LSE 38% of staff are from
EU27 countries (Talbot, 2017).

Individual disciplines have particularly strong concentra-
tions of EU staff; in economics, well over a third of academic
staff hail from the wider EU (Baker, 2017a). Britain is the
'second-most popular destination in the world for international students' (House of Commons Education Committee,
2017, p. 5) after the United States; a status facilitated by a
range of factors including the prestige of its institutions, the
place of English as a global language, and — in a significant
proportion of cases — freedom of movement proffered by the
UK's membership of the European Union. Beyond freedom of
movement, EU students also benefit from European Court of
Justice (ECJ) anti-discrimination rulings which ensure they

are entitled to equal treatment to UK students in terms of fee and loan regimes, giving them access to the UK's student finance system and fees charged at the home rate (House of Commons Education Committee, 2017, p. 8). Universities UK estimated in 2016 that EU students 'generate £3.7bn' in terms of income 'for the [wider] UK economy' (Universities UK, 2016a).

EU staff are critical to the research base, as we shall see in more detail in Chapter Three. Sir Mark Walport, then-Government Chief Scientific Adviser, and now Chief Executive of UKRI, told the House of Lords Select Committee on Science and Technology the following in advance of the referendum:

> At the moment, 30% of European Research Council
> grantees working in the UK come from other
> Member States; and 15% of UK academic staff are
> from continental Europe, which compares with 11%
> of the whole of non-EU, so not only the funding but
> the people are very important. (House of Lords
> Science and Technology Commitee, 2016, p. 50)

EU staff make up larger proportions of the academic body in particular disciplines. In 2017, 36% of staff in modern languages are citizens of EU27 countries, as were over a quarter of physicists and chemical engineers (Baker, 2017a). There remains a fear that universities could find themselves 'vulnerable' to a post-'Brexit brain drain' (Baker, 2017b). The Irish Government, to name one example, has put aside an 'unspecified' amount to attract UK-based researchers unsettled by Brexit (House of Commons Education Committee, 2017, p. 15). Pre-referendum, the reliance of Britain's universities on talent from the wider EU had been increasing, rather than lessening. The number of EU27 academics working in the United Kingdom had risen by 29% in the three years up to

2016 (Baker, 2017b). Sector-wide, the number of EU27 staff had increased by 10,000 over the six years to 2017 (House of Commons Education Committee, 2017, p. 13). Some of the increases at individual institutions were even more dramatic. At Warwick, the number of EU27 academics had risen by 70% (Baker, 2017b). International staff (including EU27 staff) are also well-represented amongst research-only staff. This is exacerbated by their critical significance to 'subjects of strategic importance' such as maths where they make up two-thirds of research-only staff (66%), economics (69%), chemical engineering (65%) and electrical, electronic and computer engineering (62%) (Universities UK, 2016a, 2016b, p. 4).

But the numbers and scale of EU27 involvement in teaching and learning in Britain's universities isn't limited to simply EU27 academics teaching in British institutions or EU27 students studying in them. Britain's 'home' staff and students are also exposed to the Europeanisation of Britain's higher education sector through a myriad of other means, not least the ERASMUS student (and, since 1997, staff) exchange programme launched in 1987 (European Union, 2012). In the past three decades, over 200,000 British students have studied in Europe under the provisions of the scheme (Vulliamy, 2016). In total, around three million EU citizens have studied abroad because of the existence of ERASMUS (European Commission, 2014a, p. 6), and as a result of that it is estimated that a million 'Erasmus' babies have been born (Green C., 2014).

However, even prior to Brexit, the place of international students within UK universities (let alone EU students) was not uncontroversial. When Home Secretary, Theresa May had championed a series of initiatives intended to decrease the number of international students in the United Kingdom, notably through the tightening of visa restrictions, initiatives which have (for example) halved the number of Indian students studying in the United Kingdom in the past seven years (House of Commons Education Committee, 2017, p. 12). May had also argued that universities should revise their business model away from international students — displaying a casual ignorance of the international dynamic underpinning the UK higher education sector (Cook, 2015). Despite consistent polling evidence that British voters did not consider students to be 'immigrants' (Kaur, 2017), the government mooted further significant curbs to student migration in the post-Brexit period. As the Scientists for EU co-founder, Rob Davidson, noted, these were 'a type of migrant no-one has a problem with apart from Theresa May' (Davidson, 2017).

This was politics over economics; May's Conservative Party had remained committed to her predecessor David Cameron's target to reduce net migration to the United Kingdom to the 'tens of thousands' (Maidment, 2017). UK higher education was an area where numbers could, potentially, be curbed efficaciously, irrespective of the consequences to institutions or the wider economy. In October 2016, newly appointed Home Secretary Amber Rudd went further in a speech to the Conservative Party conference. After commending her predecessor (the Prime Minister) for addressing the 'abuse of student visas', she outlined in more detail the implications of immigration reform for higher education:

> We will also look for the first time at whether our student immigration rules should be tailored to the quality of the course and the quality of the educational institution. I'm proud that we have world-leading centres of academic excellence. It's a testament to our country's proud history and our top universities' ability to evolve.

But the current system allows all students, irrespective of their talents and the university's quality, favourable employment prospects when they stop studying. While an international student is studying here, their family members can do any form of work. And foreign students, even those studying English Language degrees, don't even have to be proficient in speaking English.

We need to look at whether this one size fits all approach really is right for the hundreds of different universities, providing thousands of different courses across the country. And we need to look at whether this generous offer for all universities is really adding value to our economy. I'm passionately committed to making sure our world-leading institutions can attract the brightest and the best.

But a student immigration system that treats every student and university as equal only punishes those we should want to help. So, our consultation will ask what more can we do to support our best universities — and those that stick to the rules — to attract the best talent ... while looking at tougher rules for students on lower quality courses.

This isn't about pulling up the drawbridge. It's about making sure students that come here, come to study. (Rudd, 2016)

May's agenda on international and EU students was supported by the right-wing press; *The Sun* newspaper ran a story in March 2017 — the month May triggered Article 50, beginning the formal Brexit process — demonising EU 'degree-mobile' students as 'EU THIEVING STUDENTS', drawing attention to issues surrounding non-payment of tuition fees (Dathan, 2017). In August 2017, *The Sunday Times* ran a story (ultimately revealed to have been based on distorted figures and an incorrect reading of statistics) which claimed that home students were being forced out of British universities to make way for international students who paid higher fees (Gilligan, 2017; Morris D., 2017a). With EU students soon to be reclassified as international students post-Brexit, anti-international student sentiment has clear implications for British universities' European dimension. The intransigence of government policy in this area may yet shift, however. In late August 2017, the Office for National Statistics revealed that the estimates for students overstaying and abusing their visa status, which had been used to justify the Home Office's tough stance on international student visas throughout May's tenure as Home Secretary and into Rudd's, were false (Stewart, 2017). Not only were they false, but spectacularly so. Whereas the Office for National Statistics (ONS) had estimated that the number of students overstaying their visas ran into the hundreds of thousands, it transpired on the introduction of new counting methods that the actual number was fewer than 5000, meaning that over 97% of student visa holders had complied with the terms of their visa. At time of writing, the government has referred the question of student migration to a review (Stewart, Mason, & Grierson, 2017).

Universities' fears of a 'brain drain' had merit. In the first year after the referendum, 1300 EU27 staff left the United Kingdom (Savage M., 2017). The House of Commons Education Committee inquiry cited a UCU survey on the prevailing mood amongst EU27 academics:

> Over three-quarters (76%) of EU academics at UK universities said that, due to the referendum result, they were now more likely to consider leaving UK

higher education. A *Times Higher Education* poll in March 2017 of academics found that 53% of non-UK nationals were 'actively looking to leave the UK' and 88% said that the prospect of Brexit has made them more likely to do so in the medium- to long-term … Although an objection to the 'hostile current climate' caused by the referendum result was cited as the main reason, 40% of respondents also cited fears over their future immigration status. (House of Commons Education Committee, 2017, p. 14)

STAFF, STUDENTS AND FREEDOM OF MOVEMENT

EU27 staff found themselves in a particularly difficult situation post-referendum. Their status as eligible to work in the United Kingdom rested on the same 'fundamental' freedom of EU membership as student mobility, namely freedom of movement. The Brexit vote did not in itself mean an end to freedom of movement, but the post-vote policy approach of the May government and the Corbyn-led opposition did — in the 2017 General Election campaign both main parties accepted that freedom of movement would come to an end, with clear implications for a potential reduction in immigration from the EU to the UK.

This begged the question of what would happen to EU27 citizens resident and working in the United Kingdom, including EU27 academics. The eventual UK offer — which took a year to appear — to EU residents in the United Kingdom was branded by one Russell Group vice-chancellor as 'derisory' (Croft, 2017), requiring EU residents to apply for 'settled status' once they had completed a five-year qualifying period

(Yeo, 2017). The EU proposal for British citizens in the rest of the EU was considerably more generous, allowing current rights in perpetuity regardless of documentation or qualifying period, and extending these rights to family members (BBC News, 2017a). Despite the government's attempts to downplay the sector's anxieties, there is a consensus amongst university leaders and research bodies that the Brexit vote has hit Britain's attractiveness as an international recruiter, with institutions reporting that highly-skilled candidates from overseas had withdrawn from consideration or rejected job offers following the outcome (Russell Group, 2016). EU27 staff reported an increase in xenophobia which paralleled the post-referendum surge in hate crime (Johnston, 2016). In the words of Warwick's vice-chancellor, Stuart Croft:

> Where you're sitting now I have staff telling me I don't know what the future of my child is. It doesn't get more fundamental than that, I don't think, in terms of making people feel they're not wanted and unclear about whether they're going to commit to keep on working in this country or not; 'I don't know whether my child can stay here or not'. So, it's taken the government twelve months to make a fairly derisory offer, in terms of non-British EU citizens and their future in this country, so really difficult, really difficult … (Croft, 2017)

Though his institution, Warwick, had 'not lost many' EU27 staff at time of writing, Croft noted that 'we have lost some'. Interestingly, those expressing concerns did not just leave for the continent:

> … some that we have lost we have actually lost to other parts of the UK, where people say to me and to others that they feel more comfortable and are

> more cosmopolitan places than this part of the
> Midlands, London of course in particular, but also
> Manchester. (Croft, 2017)

EU27 academics fears were heightened, when, in August 2017, the Home Office erroneously sent 100 letters to EU nationals resident in the United Kingdom stating they would be 'detained' prior to 'deportation' (Moore-Bridger, 2017). One was the Finnish historian, Dr Eva Holmberg, who told the *Evening Standard* that:

> It makes you feel like you are being treated like a
> common criminal … This absurd nonsense has aged
> me at least five years and made me even less likely to
> trust anything Amber Rudd, Theresa May, or David
> Davis says to calm us EU nationals down. It shows
> the home office currently cannot function. It does
> not know how to obey the law or even its own rules.
> It is probably not able to deal with all the paper-
> work. (Moore-Bridger, 2017)

The House of Commons Education Select Committee argued that the United Kingdom should seek to unilaterally guarantee the status of academic staff, and to ensure special provisions within any forthcoming immigration reform:

> The immigration system after Brexit should cater
> more particularly for the needs of higher education.
> It should facilitate, rather than obstruct, movement
> of people from and to our universities. An easier
> route than Tier 2 for academics from across the
> globe, with a less bureaucracy, is necessary. (House
> of Commons Education Committee, 2017, p. 3)

The 'easier route than Tier 2' was, and remains, of critical importance. The reclassification of EU staff as 'international' has serious implications. Though the government's offer may potentially mitigate some of the problems they may face, it does not equate to the present terms and has implications for the future recruitment of EU27 staff. With regard to existing staff, the Russell Group noted that of their EU27 staff (academic and professional), only just over a quarter of them would meet the current threshold criterion of an annual salary of £30,000 or above (Russell Group, 2016, p. 8).

On the student front, ECJ rulings ensure that European citizens cannot be discriminated against in favour of 'home students': this means that EU27 'credit-mobile' students seeking to study in the United Kingdom are entitled to access the same financial support and fee regime as UK home student (James, 2016, p. 10). In practice, this has the effect of making UK study relatively more attractive than it might otherwise be; this means that EU students have the ability to access the tuition fee loans system (something nearly two-thirds of them availed themselves of in 2014/2015) (House of Commons Education Committee, 2017, p. 8). Thus EU students are able to defer the effect of fees in the same manner as UK students, which means that the otherwise potential disincentive of the UK's comparatively high fees (by European standards) is mitigated. As the Provost of UCL, Michel Arthur noted in relation to his institution:

> More than 1,700 of UCL's EU students are under-graduates who until now have been eligible for the £9,000 tuition fees that home students pay — and the associated loan scheme — which is significantly cheaper than fees for other international students. It's difficult to imagine a government that's just exited from Europe wishing to continue the loan scheme for EU students. (Arthur, 2016)

Were EU students liable for reclassification as 'international' students, then the international students fee regime would apply — where fees have no set limit and students do not have access to the UK tuition fee loans system. A decline in EU27 student numbers has profound political, economic and cultural implications both for Britain's universities but also UK society as a whole. At the political level, a 2015 HEPI analysis found that international students were a significant form of 'soft power' for the United Kingdom (HEPI, 2015a). At that time, 55 heads of state or government were alumni of UK institutions, including (within the EU) the Presidents of Ireland, Belgium and Cyprus, the Prime Ministers of Portugal, Hungary and Malta and the Queen of Denmark (HEPI, 2015b). At the economic level, as we have seen EU students are estimated to bring in £3.7bn to the wider UK economy, supporting around 34,000 jobs nationwide (House of Commons Education Committee, 2017, p. 9). This is of particular significance in specific parts of the United Kingdom; in Scotland, for example, EU students make up a larger proportion of international students than in the United Kingdom as a whole. Gerry McCormac, Principal of Strling University, notes that 'over 50,000 [international students] choose to study in Scotland, and of these 21,000 are from the EU — the highest proportion in the UK.' (McCormac, 2016). The greater proportion of EU27 students in Scotland may be at least in part attributable to the greater generosity of the fees regime there, where EU27 students are treated the same as Scottish ones — paying no fees at all — unlike their English counterparts. At time of writing, the Scottish Government has guaranteed the continuation of this offer for EU students beginning courses in 2018 (McIvor, 2017). It remains to be seen what position will be adopted for those students beginning courses in 2019 and beyond.

At a cultural level, EU27 students contribute to an essential part of undergraduate education, namely 'cultural exchange' (McCormac, 2016). As McCormac puts it:

> The richness of experience and mutual understanding of cultural differences provided by young people from across Europe, who live and learn together, is immeasurable. Given Europe's history of war and conflict, it's uplifting to see young people exploring different cultures learning together. (McCormac, 2016)

A HEPI research paper underlined the appeal of learning alongside international students for UK home applicants to university, noting that for 87% of applicants this would 'give them a better world view', with 85% claiming it to be 'useful preparation for working in a global environment' and over three-quarters arguing it would 'help them develop a global network' (HEPI, 2015c).

There is evidence that the events of the Brexit moment have already provided an active disincentive to EU27 staff and students to come to the United Kingdom. The UK government confirmed that EU entrants to UK higher education would have access to the UK higher education (HE) student financial system for the duration of their courses, but this was only announced 'three days before the 11 October application deadline' for Oxford, Cambridge and the medical schools (House of Commons Education Committee, 2017, p. 10). This had serious implications; Cambridge saw a 14% drop in applications from the EU as a result of the uncertainty (Trinity College, Cambridge, 2017). There was a 9% fall overall of EU27 students applying for the early deadline institutions (Weale, 2016). There was a 5% fall in EU applications overall, which contributed to the 'first fall in UK university applications since 2012', the first year of the post-Browne fees regime (Walker & Warrell, 2017). Current UK students expressed their own fears of the potential impact of the Brexit moment to the Education Select Committee inquiry. This was one response selected from a focus group of students at the University of Leeds, who had made a submission as part of a parliamentary studies scheme:

> I think that there is cause for concern with moving out of [the] EU — we may lose interest from European students. This will reduce diversity which is important in building a strong learning community and also money. This brings in further danger of higher fees, heading towards similar expense that we see in America. (House of Commons Education. Committee, 2017, p. 36)

The editors of the submission claimed that:

> half of our EU respondents expressed [the view that] the referendum result had impacted negatively upon their considerations of studying in the UK; half expressing [the view] that it had no effect; no respondent expressed a positive effect. (House of Commons Education Committee, 2017, p. 36)

Reading's student submission for its part put forward the following prospectus, most of which would subsequently be rendered impossible by the government's chosen negotiating stance: 'Keep Erasmus, stay in the single market, [keep] freedom of movement and right-to-work protection; protection of current international students' (House of Commons Education Committee, 2017, p. 38). Students were aware of the potential threat to staff:

> By leaving the EU, the UK runs the risk of insulating its universities from the international academic

> community. It is imperative that freedom of move-
> ment is maintained so that researchers and aca-
> demics can move freely into the UK from Europe,
> thereby contributing to the quality of third level
> education in the UK. (Begley, 2016)

A number of students expressed concern about the potential implications of Brexit on the attractiveness and availability of modern languages courses. Many such courses feature in-country placements in EU member states facilitated by the ERASMUS programme; the possibility ending of UK participation in the scheme gave rise to concerns that modern languages courses would no longer be an attractive proposition:

> The number of students doing a foreign language
> degree is already quite low and this uncertainty
> around Brexit, means that potential language stu-
> dents may be put off a language degree as they are
> unsure whether or not they will spend their third
> year abroad, which will only further lead to a
> decline in language graduates in the UK. (Davies J.,
> 2016)

Students also highlighted a potential issue of exclusion due to cost:

> Without maintaining participation of the Erasmus
> programme, it will be extremely difficult for lan-
> guage students from low-income families (such as
> myself) to complete the compulsory third year
> abroad of their degree. (Green J., 2016)

> If the Erasmus grant is no longer available to British
> students, and if they have to begin to pay for visas
> to study or work elsewhere in Europe, a great num-
> ber of students will find that these opportunities are

unaffordable. International mobility will be reserved
only for the elite. (Williams, 2016)

One former ERASMUS student and former officer of the
ERASMUS student network flagged up his fears for the place
of EU staff and students in the UK, citing his fear of rising
'xenophobia' and the stabbing of a Polish student from
Portsmouth University:

> [It] is also worth mentioning the recent attacks on
> EU nationals studying in the UK, such as that experi-
> enced by Bartosz Milewski of Portsmouth
> University. As somebody who has spent much of my
> adult life helping international and exchange stu-
> dents to interact with and contribute to local British
> communities, I feel sickened that the divisive and
> poorly run referendum campaign has emboldened
> the racist and xenophobic in society to behave in
> this way towards foreign students, amongst others
> of course … (Huitson, 2016)

ERASMUS represents a juncture between political conceptions of citizenship, academic ideas of internationalism and
the legal framework which underpins both. As a potential
casualty of the Brexit moment with real implications for both
staff and students, it is worth examining in more depth.

MOBILITY: THE CASE OF ERASMUS

The ERASMUS scheme, established in 1987 at a time
of 'unusual political promotion' for 'student mobility'
(Papatsiba, 2005, p. 173), represents an opportunity for
students within the EU to undertake part of their studies
in another member state. Around 16,000 British students

annually make use of the scheme to study in a range of EU27 countries (UK Erasmus+ National Agency, 2016). The current iteration of the programme, ERASMUS+, incorporates staff exchanges alongside student ones, seeking to build pedagogical knowledge transfer around member states (British Council, 2017).

The ERASMUS scheme began during the 1980s attempt to construct a 'social Europe', at a time when some scholars believe the integration project to have been in the doldrums (Bickerton, 2016). Alongside attempts to liberalise the trading regime came the push for a social Europe:

> For those left-wing parties who found themselves out of power, building a 'social Europe' seemed more realistic than trying to stem the tide of neoliberalism at home. (Bickerton, 2016)

ERASMUS (more formally the European Region Action Scheme for the Mobility of University Students) became characteristic of academic attempts to 'capture' ostensibly economic policies in favour of more 'academic' agendas (Papatsiba, 2005). The ERASMUS+ mandate today is couched in the classic terminology of the knowledge economy:

> Erasmus+ is the EU Programme in the fields of education, training, youth and sport for the period 2014-2021. Education, training, youth and sport can make a major contribution to help tackle socioeconomic changes, the key challenges that Europe will be facing until the end of the decade and to support the implementation of the European policy agenda for growth, jobs, equity and social inclusion. Fighting rising levels of unemployment — particularly among young people — has become one of the most urgent tasks for European governments. Too

many young people leave school prematurely running a high risk of being unemployed and socially
marginalised. The same risk threatens many adults
with low skills. Technologies are changing the way
in which society operates, and there is a need to
ensure the best use is made of them. EU businesses
need to become more competitive through talent and
innovation ... (European Commission, 2016, p. 5)

Like all programmes, ERASMUS+ requires funding — to the
tune of €14.7 billion in the current cycle (a 40% increase on
the previous one) — and thus flags up policymaker-friendly
growth-oriented objectives (Grove, 2013). But lower down
the ERASMUS+ list of priorities comes the following:

Europe needs more cohesive and inclusive societies
which allow citizens to play an active role in democratic life. Education and youth work are key to
promote common European values, foster social
integration, enhance intercultural understanding
and a sense of belonging to a community, and
to prevent violent radicalisation. (European
Commission, 2016, p. 5)

This is the current iteration of a sentiment from the 1980s
whereby policymakers at the European level sought to
promote an idea of 'European citizenship' through the
ERASMUS scheme. The legal dimension of European citizenship became of significance to a wider clientele than
ERASMSUS students when the Maastricht Treaty codified it,
with subsequent non-discrimination rulings allowing students
within the EU a greater opportunity to become 'degree
mobile' as well as 'credit mobile' within the EU. This was
because their EU citizenship now conferred the right to
receive the same preferential financial settlements offered to

'home' students. This meant it would be easier for EU students to take their whole degree in other EU states. In the 10 years from 2004, the number of EU students studying at universities in the UK rose by 32% (Universities UK, 2015, p. 17). The legal settlement which facilitated this increase is what Grant characterises as the 'first register' of citizenship, that of legal rights and obligations (Grant, 2016b). But ERASMUS, which represents 'credit mobile' rather than 'degree mobile' students, had an ambition in Grant's second register — that of belonging (Grant, 2016b). As Papatsiba puts it, one of the political ambitions of ERASMUS from its early stages was a desire to foster 'a means to reach international understanding and create a European consciousness' (Papatsiba, 2005, p. 174). This was part of a broader agenda on the part of European bodies to develop 'European identity', as Audrey Osler notes (Osler, 1998, p. 77). As Iain Wilson notes, the attempt to foster European identity through ERASMUS is real, notwithstanding the often ostensibly economic values included in policy texts (Wilson, 2011). Instead, the ambiguity within the texts reflects the nature of the policy process, and the need to assemble 'coalitions':

> One of the difficulties of evaluating the Erasmus programme is that its declared objectives have changed repeatedly throughout its history ... In order for ideas such as supporting student mobility within the EU to become programmes, coalitions have to be formed in support of them. The members of these coalitions may have different objectives but want to do the same things to achieve them. Some might wish to increase political support for the EU, while others may wish to improve the employability of European graduates. (Wilson, 2011, p. 1116)

In Wilson's view, 'while some of Erasmus' sponsors did see it primarily as a means to economic and educational ends, their importance may have been overstated for political convenience'; this was how it was 'sold to member states' (Wilson, 2011, p. 1118). It didn't change the fact that the fundamental agenda was to 'promote ... student mobility within the EU largely on the assumption that mobile students will become more pro-European' (Wilson, 2011, p. 1113).

Though clearly a 'political project', this was in keeping with post-war academic sentiment which saw international exchanges as a fundamental mechanism of socialisation and conflict-prevention.[1]

ERASMUS has never been a perfect scheme, either from the perspective of the United Kingdom or its European partners. The United Kingdom has sent relatively fewer of its students abroad than might be expected for a higher education system of its size; in recent years it has received at least twice as many students as it has sent (Gibbs, 2014). This is, in a sense, illustrative of Britain's unique place within Europe. British students are less likely than their European peers to have engaged with foreign languages, and this is an integral factor in their underparticipation in ERASMUS (Curtis, 2004). British ERASMUS participation has been heavily weighted in favour of modern languages students using the scheme to complete compulsory in-country requirements, or seeking to broaden their language base (James, 2016, p. 17).

As for the 'political project', even amongst a sample of French students, ERASMUS appeared to only in part — if at all — fulfil the goals of bolstering a keener sense of European identity (Papatsiba, 2005). Students reporting in this study tended instead to see ERASMUS in terms of their individual benefit in terms of their human capital development (Papatsiba, 2005). Insofar as ERASMUS students are pro-European, Wilson finds this isn't to do with the impact of

ERASMUS on participating students — but merely a reflection of the fact that applicants to the scheme have 'unusually pro-European views' (Wilson, 2011, p. 1135). And though staff across the continent have been keen to use ERASMUS provisions to facilitate their own exchanges abroad, the ambitions of the early days have had to be constrained in light of the prevailing dissimilarity of European higher education systems, notwithstanding the Bologna Process (Enders, 1998, p. 47).

Though UK universities are certainly international in outlook and increasingly European in orientation — and keen to defend the UK's continued participation in ERASMUS — this is not to say that ERASMUS has been an unvarnished success story for the United Kingdom (though it is clearly fundamental to modern languages programmes). Yet UK students and alumni participating in, or having participated in the scheme are staunch defenders of it. One student from Northern Ireland told the House of Commons Education Committee offered a representative comment:

> It's very important that the UK maintains its
> Erasmus membership as there are so many students
> from across the UK that get to have an incredible
> year abroad because of it. So many of my friends
> from University are undertaking years abroad in
> places like France and Spain, and this simply isn't
> financially possible without Erasmus funding. It's
> hard to describe what meeting people from so many
> different cultures does to you, but it has impacted
> me in such a positive way … I believe firmly that
> Erasmus is vital to the University experience for so
> many UK students, without it we would not broaden
> our horizons, have new experiences, learn different

> languages, see a different corner of the
> world … (Hegan, 2016)

He also noted his fears for the Irish common travel area and
the dangers posed by Brexit for the Northern Irish peace settlement; 'none of us want to return to the borders of the past
I'm told about' (Hegan, 2016).

It may be worth thinking of ERASMUS counterfactually;
in its absence, the situation with UK-European exchange
would be markedly worse, as ERASMUS provides funding
directly to the student to support them in their host country,
often at nominal cost in terms of tuition (indeed, UK students
often benefit from superior student finance systems abroad to
those prevailing in their home country). In practical terms
then this means that the withdrawal of the United Kingdom
from ERASMUS would likely have a significant impact on
the study abroad opportunities available to UK students. But
it would not be limited to merely this. The recategorisation of
EU students as international ones would impact on the numbers who would choose the United Kingdom as a destination
for study outside ERASMUS, and the non-existence of the
former ERASMUS network (as far as the United Kingdom is
concerned) coupled with the UK government's insistence on
tighter visa restrictions for international students, represents
a 'perfect storm' for credit-mobile and degree-mobile
students.

This has major implications for the educational opportunities available to UK students in a home setting, as witnesses
to the House of Commons Education Select Committee
noted:

> Birkbeck, University of London, said fewer EU
> students in England 'may lead to a loss of cross-
> cultural fertilisation of ideas and culture on our

campuses.' Sorana Vieru, Vice-President for Higher
Education at the National Union of Students (NUS),
said that EU students challenge perspectives, enrich
the overall university experience and help home
students develop new views. (House of Commons
Education Committee, 2017, p. 10)

Intercultural education taking place in and out of the class-
room is, to some degree, an intangible benefit of undergraduate education, one which ERASMUS supports. The closure of
this mechanism plus government pressure on international
students more generally restricts not merely the movement of
EU students, but the quality of education UK home students
receive. As one respondent to the House of Commons inquiry
put it, there would

be a negative effect on learning outcomes for
students through less opportunities to see the
World from a variety of perspectives thanks [to] the
phenomenon of 'Internationalisation at Home'.
(Huitson, 2016)

In the whirlwind of reform which has characterised the past
several decades of higher education policy in the United
Kingdom, accentuated by recent rhetoric around 'disruption'
and virtual learning, the insights of the 1957 Niblett Report
on residence have been forgotten — that much of the benefit
of an undergraduate education accrues from residence, and
the interaction with others which promotes cultural exchange
and openness (University Grants Committee, 1957). This is
not a feature of higher education which is amenable to
'metrics'.

UK ERASMUS alumni viewed the possible demise of the
UK's participation in the scheme as a generational 'injustice',

in keeping with broader sentiments on the supposed-break-down of the intergenerational contract:

> The idea that future generations of students may not
> be able to participate in the Erasmus programme to
> the same capacity — if at all — is an injustice. It is
> important that Britain maintains its Erasmus mem-
> bership so that students continue to have the oppor-
> tunity to grow and learn within an environment that
> UK universities alone cannot provide. (Begley, 2016)

CONCLUSIONS

The Brexit moment has profound implications for the staff and students of the UK's universities. On the one hand, it may change their very makeup, as EU27 staff and students either leave the United Kingdom or elect to study elsewhere. Amongst EU27 staff, there has an element of fear, with regard to their right of remain in the United Kingdom and the changing political climate. The historian of citizenship Matthew Grant, writing in the referendum's aftermath, puts the grounds for such fears pithily:

> In post-referendum Britain, the shrinking sense of
> belonging is palpable. As the history of debates on
> citizenship shows, when an individual, group or
> community is no longer considered to belong,
> attacks on their rights, their position, and their
> bodies soon follow (Grant, 2016a).

Citizenship is the fulcrum of the debate on the implications of the Brexit moment for British universities' staff and students. On the one hand, there is the question of academic citizen-ship, which belongs to Grant's second 'register' of citizenship, belonging. Within the academic community, EU programmes such as ERASMUS, operate at the interface between Grant's first and second registers of citizenship — the legal and the communal dimensions (Grant, 2016a). The legal dimension of European citizenship, afforded by the Maastricht Treaty in 1992, facilitated the exercise of academic citizenship, in the shape of greater interaction within the borderless world of education. Brexit ruptured the legal and political foundations of this world. As in other sectors, the relationship between Brexit and university staff and students is a reflexive one. UK students protested against Brexit shortly after the referendum result was known, and a survey held after the referendum highlighted that 'three-quarters of students' were 'angry' about the result (Havergal, 2016). One survey respondent described the United Kingdom as 'xenophobic and racist' (Havergal, 2016), whilst a respondent to the Education Committee inquiry described it as 'closed and non-progressive' (Green J., 2016). EU27 staff who sought to secure their position after the Brexit vote found that their experience mirrored the macropolitics of UK immigration policy. As Colin Talbot noted, after the referendum

> [S]ome EU academics … decided … they should try to cement their position by applying for one or other of the various routes to permanent residency. The procedures are daunting and of Kafkaesque complexity — one form runs to 85 pages and requires forms of proof that make acquiring Catholic sainthood look simple. (Talbot, 2017)

One of Talbot's respondents put it bluntly: 'the Home Office is hedging its bets because we non-UK [academics] are now effectively hostages' (Talbot, 2017). The exodus of EU staff since the referendum has been felt at a range of institutions, and the possibility of restrictions of student mobility poses real logistical questions for institutions around the United Kingdom, especially those delivering modern languages courses. As the students cited here have noted, any failure to secure equivalent arrangements for student mobility will run the risk of student mobility becoming an exercise of privilege, rather than the subsidised right it has hitherto been within the EU framework. Whilst the Brexit moment has implications for staff and students, this is also an area where it has impacts — and where the effect of these is already discernible. Despite the rage for capital projects and building programmes in the Browne era, universities are fundamentally communities of students and staff. They conceive of themselves as belonging to a wider, non-territorial, intellectual community in a 'borderless' world. The end of freedom of movement will fundamentally reorient the UK element of this world. As one UK student put it after the referendum, 'England feels so much more of an island than it did before' (Havergal, 2016). For staff, freedom of movement was critical to the pursuit of intellectual inquiry and collaboration with staff from the other 27 member-states, collaborations which have now been thrown into jeopardy in the Brexit moment, and it is to these that we turn to next.

NOTE

1. See Chapter Three.

CHAPTER THREE

RESEARCH AND FUNDING

It will not only be commodities which travel, but also ideas which will have wings. When fiscal and commercial barriers will have been abolished between different states, as they have already been between the provinces of the same state; when different countries, in daily relations, tend towards the unity of peoples, how will you be able to revive the old mode of separation?

— François-René Chateaubriand, cited in Emma Rothschild (Summer, 1999).

The EU, imperfect though it is, has been a spur to collaboration...[it is hard to believe] that European scientists, still operating in a common space, would look to Britain to collaborate ... It is difficult to believe that the UK science budget would be increased post-Brexit to compensate for lost EU funding.

— Chris Husbands, Vice-Chancellor, Sheffield Hallam University and Chair of the TEF, cited in Mike Finn (2016a)

Underlying [Brexit] is the basic gap that now exists
between people who can imagine a viable future
for themselves in a networked world, and those
who cannot. Cambridge is a networked town
par excellence: socially, digitally, economically.
University towns voted overwhelmingly to remain,
often as outliers in regions that wanted to leave:
Newcastle in the North East, Warwick in the
West Midlands, Exeter in the South West, Norwich
in East Anglia. By contrast, many parts of the UK
appear to feel that the vital connections that drive
the flow of money and power in the 21st century
are increasingly passing them by. The EU is
symptomatic of this sense of exclusion, but it is
not the cause.

— David Runciman (2016a)

THE EUROPEAN UNION, NETWORKS AND THE 'REPUBLIC OF SCIENCE'

In 1962, the Hungarian-born British chemist Michael Polanyi, Former professor of physical chemistry at the University of Manchester, penned an influential article for the journal *Minerva* (Polanyi, 1962). Entitled 'The Republic of Science: Its Political and Economic Theory', Polanyi's article traced an outline of what he conceived the international scientific community to be, and its purpose. He believed that the scientific community was 'organised in a way which resembles certain features of a body politic and works according to economic principles similar to those by which the production of material goods is regulated' (Polanyi, 1962, p. 54).

More than this, the scientific community could be a 'model' for a 'free society':

> For in the free co-operation of independent scientists we shall find a highly-simplified model of a free society, which presents in isolation certain basic features of it that are more difficult to identify within the comprehensive functions of a national body.
> (Polanyi, 1962, p. 54)

In this, he appeared to echo C. P. Snow, who some years earlier had referred (approvingly) to a 'culture' of science:

> The scientific culture really is a culture, not only in an intellectual but an anthropological sense. That is, its members need not, and of course, often do not, always completely understand each other … but there are common attitudes, common standards and patterns of behaviour, common approaches and assumptions. It cuts across other mental patterns, such as those of religion or politics or class. (Snow, 1961, p. 10)

Science for Polanyi was an international community, for Snow an international culture. Snow's thesis has come in for much (justified) criticism, both by contemporaries and historians (Edgerton, 2005; Leavis, 2013 [1962]; Ortolano, 2009). But the international dimension of science was something he shared with Polanyi. Their reflections imply shared understandings of academic citizenship, and for Polanyi at least this was by no means limited to natural scientists. Academics and intellectuals in general were citizens not simply of their nation, but the world.

These notions of international academic citizenship, of scholarly and scientific communities which transcended the arbitrariness of national boundaries, have been characteristic of the development of the modern university, but they have not been restricted to the natural sciences. They have not been dependent on the existence of the European Union, either. As Ulrike Kircheberger notes, 'there existed close connections between scientific institutions in Britain and Germany throughout the nineteenth century', not to mention 'strong ties between classicists in Gottingen and at the universities of Oxford and Cambridge' (Ellis & Kircheberger, 2014, p. 4). Refugees, immigrants and the children of immigrants were critical to the development of the post-war British university. Polanyi was one such. Frederick Lindemann, a German-born Oxford physicist (subsequently ennobled as Viscount Cherwell), whose father had immigrated to Britain in the 1870s, was another (Fort, 2003). He became an evangelist for British scientific and technological education both within and without government, where he twice served at Winston Churchill's behest as scientific adviser and Paymaster General (Fort, 2003). Karl Popper, who came to the United Kingdom via New Zealand as a refugee from Nazi persecution, became a pivotal figure in the London School of Economics' philosophy department, and articulated a keen vision of the scientific community's self-image (Popper, 2002 [1959]). His political philosophy also played a key role in Lionel Robbins' thinking on the role of universities in society. When Robbins, now one of the preeminent educationalists in Europe, went to Gottingen in 1964 to pronounce to European rectors and vice-chancellors on the place of the 'university in the modern world', he condemned nationalism in language that borrowed from both Popper and Polanyi:

> [W]e must emphasise the common element in civilizations, rather than the minor variations. We must teach at all times the impersonality of knowledge

and the transcendence of values. We must dwell on
the universal element in the human spirit. Above all,
we should set our forces against the intrusion into
science and learning of the anti-social forces of
nationalism. Under the influence of a misguided
historicism, our universities have not been guiltless
of fostering such fissiparous tendencies. We need —
Britons, Frenchmen, Germans, all of us — to return
to the outlook and values of the *Aufklarungzeit*, to
that Enlightenment which stressed the unity of
humanity, rather than its differences. Without weak-
ening the sense of duty to their local society, we
must seek to make our young men and women citizens of that republic of mind which knows no
frontiers. (Robbins L., 1966b, p. 16)

Historicism was Popper, whilst the 'republic of mind' owed a
debt to Polanyi. These were the sentiments at the heart of
Robbins' own report into the British higher education system
of a year earlier (Committee on Higher Education, 1963).
The Robbins Report did not initiate university expansion,
but it stood as a representative mission statement for its
nature (Committee on Higher Education, 1963). The frontierless 'republic of mind' was essential to it, and whilst Robbins
was keen to emphasise universities' links to their 'local societies', he was wary of that being constructed in nationalist
terms.

Academic networks — arguably the most significant
aspect of the EU's involvement in higher education — predated the EU. Leave supporters in the United Kingdom have
taken this to mean that Britain's forthcoming exit from the
EU will have little impact on universities, which supposedly
can simply buy back in to whichever aspects of the EU higher
education settlement they wish (a belief that is far from

well-founded, as we shall see). But this misses the essential point that since the advent of the European Union, Polanyi's 'republic of science' and Popper's 'republic of mind' — if they can be thought of as the same concept, namely an international academic community without barriers — has been facilitated and institutionalised by the EU itself. According to Jonathan Adams, the 'rise' of networks in scientific research represents a 'fundamental shift ... in the geography of science' as scientific networks around the world become increasingly regionalised (Adams, 2012, p. 335). For the United Kingdom, it has particular implications:

> Papers with hundreds of co-authors contribute to the apparent pervasiveness of collaboration between countries. For example, every country in Europe co-authors with every other country in the region. For the United Kingdom and Germany, this collaboration is relatively intense and represents many individual links. In 2011, the two countries had around 10,000 joint publications in journals indexed on Thomson Reuters' Web of Science — double the total in 2003 and about 10% of each country's total output. (Adams, 2012, p. 335)

Such works pack more of a punch too, at least according to traditional 'metrics'; 'publications with international co-authorship are on average more highly-cited than UK domestic ones' (Adams, 2017, p. 3). Adams (writing long before Brexit) offers a sobering reflection: 'It is difficult to go your own way in a village, even one that is global' (Adams, 2012, p. 336). As Chris Bickerton notes, the foundation of the European Communities themselves in 1957 had science at its centre, due to the inescapable fact that 'what we generally call the Treaty of Rome was in fact two treaties: the

European Economic Community [EEC] treaty and the European Atomic Energy Community [Euratom] Treaty' (Bickerton, 2016). Euratom has become a highly-controversial aspect of the Brexit process, with the government's intention to leave raising the prospect of Parliamentary rebellions (Asthana, Stewart, & Vaughan, 2017). But at this point in our discussion it is worth simply noting that scientific research in particular was written into the EU settlement from the very outset. We will return to Euratom later.

Though scientific research often dominates these discussions, such 'ecosystems' exist in the arts and humanities too. To cite but one example, the Cambridge Centre for Research for the Arts, Social Sciences and Humanities (CRASSH) has been the beneficiary of ERC grant funding to support its endeavours, but it has also benefited from the movement of researchers which has accompanied this funding. In April 2017, the Centre produced a short film illustrating its relationship with the ERC, which noted that Cambridge as a whole had received 218 ERC grants in the preceding 10 years (CRASSH, 2017). At CRASSH, these had supported projects such as the 'Bible and Antiquity in Nineteenth Century Culture' and 'Visual Representations of the Third Plague Pandemic'. They had also allowed humanities work to be undertaken in a dramatically different, collaborative, interdisciplinary fashion than has customarily been the case. CRASSH's Director, Professor Simon Goldhill, stated that as a 'result':

> My own work has fundamentally changed, not just
> in the subject area … but in the ability to explore
> the full scope of the sort of questions I'm interested
> in and to have the full input of twelve wonderful
> colleagues. (CRASSH, 2017)

This was a view reinforced by a respondent to the House of
Commons Education Select Committee, Professor Brian
Cummings, a literature specialist at the University of York
(Cummings, 2016). Cummings' 'major concern about the
impact of Brexit on higher education concerns a collaborative
research culture':

> In the humanities, which traditionally were seen as a
> solitary activity, this has been the most impactful
> change in academic life in the last two decades. I have
> been a partner in two long-term projects of the
> Deutsche Forschungsgemeinschaft; in another with the
> European University Institute in Italy; in another (with
> EU funding) involving partners from several countries
> including the Netherlands and France ... Not only is
> international collaboration a vital source of funding. It
> is also central to productive, creative, innovative think-
> ing. Ideas do not have borders. The changes of rela-
> tions with the EU should not be turned into an
> artificial form of limit for thought. (Cummings, 2016)

EU-sponsored networks are at the heart of the contemporary
UK university system. These have been facilitated by the 'four
freedoms' incorporated in EU membership, notably freedom
of movement, but they have also been supported by funding
through the Framework Programmes, including the much-
discussed current version — Horizon 2020 — Regional
Development Funds (RDFs) and Euratom. As the House of
Lords Science and Technology Committee put it prior to the
referendum:

> The UK's level of engagement with EU funding pro-
> grammes, for instance, is considerable. EU member-
> ship also has significant bearing on scientific
> collaborations, the mobility of researchers,

> regulatory frameworks and research and develop-
> ment (R&D) undertaken by businesses, to highlight
> just some of the interactions between EU member-
> ship and the vitality, or otherwise, of science and
> research in the UK. (House of Commons Education
> Committee, 2017, p. 4)

One such initiative is the Marie Curie-Sklodowska actions, which sponsor PhD students, early-career and later-stage researchers to take up positions within other EU member states (European Commission, 2017a, 2017b) . In August 2017, the Manchester-based physicist and Nobel Laureate Andre Geim went public with his concerns. In the wake of the Brexit vote, applications to join his renowned research group through the EU-sponsored Marie Curie scheme collapsed. As he noted in an interview with *The Independent*, in 2017 he had received no applications through the scheme at all (Parkin, 2017). For Geim, the question now was not what were the upsides and downsides of Brexit on a material level — merely, in Geim's words — 'to what extent is this now going to be a disaster for science in the UK' (Parkin, 2017). Geim gained his Nobel Prize for his work on graphene. Dubbed by the press a 'miracle material' (Ramirez, 2015), graphene is '200 times stronger than steel', and according to the Graphene Research Centre at Manchester has a range of potential applications from revolutionising desalination giving 'clean drinking water for millions' to providing new components for 'lightweight planes' (Graphene Research Centre, 2017). The Graphene Research Centre is part funded by a £23million European Regional Development Fund (ERDF) grant (Edge Hill University, 2016). Geim's research group enshrines in its very makeup the notion of a 'republic of science':

> ... he and most of his engineers are not British by
> birth. Indian and Chinese nationalities dominate,

followed by Russians, Ukrainians, Italians, Spanish
and Polish. All of his funding comes from the EU.
The Brexit result has cast thick doubt about how
money and people will flow to and from the UK.
(Parkin, 2017)

Geim's concerns point up the interconnectedness of the
issues raised for universities by the Brexit moment. His
mooted desire to leave the United Kingdom was but one of
the most high-profile examples of a growing trend. The
republic of science might have had strong foundations within
the realm of university campuses, but at a political level —
and in broader society — its values were either unknown or
wholly out of sympathy. The 'Brexit brain drain' as it became
known began almost immediately on the announcement of
the referendum's outcome, with Mike Savage, the LSE social
scientist, revealing that he had been made an offer by an
EU-based university within hours of the vote being declared
(Savage M., 2016). The international press watched with
interest; *El Pais* in Spain noted that UK universities 'contribute[d] a respectable 2.8% of GDP', and that UK-based EU27
researchers 'fel[t] unsure about their future' (Cebrián, 2017).
One vice-chancellor remarked that much depended on the
ability of the government to secure a post-Brexit deal to facilitate continued collaboration between the United Kingdom
and Europe, otherwise this could be the beginning of the end
for the UK's much-vaunted second-place to the US sector. He
predicted that in the event of no deal on science the UK
higher education and research system could slip behind rivals
including Canada, Australia and potentially China by the
2030s (Croft, 2017).

But academics weren't prepared to give up without a
fight. During the year which elapsed between the outcome
of the referendum and the actual beginning of Brexit

negotiations — a process delayed by the UK government and the Prime Minister's foolhardy decision to call a General Election having already triggered Article 50 — the research and scientific community attempted to exert influence on Whitehall in order to shape the terms of Brexit. A so-called 'soft' Brexit, implying that the United Kingdom would remain in the Customs Union and the Single Market, would ensure that the 'four freedoms' were maintained, critically including freedom of movement. Scientists and researchers were unsuccessful in their lobbying; as Geim notes, academic research is but one of the many 'casualties' of Brexit (Parkin, 2017). The Department for Exiting the EU (DExEU) under David Davis elected not to appoint a Scientific Adviser (Else, 2017a). BEIS under Jo Johnson's aegis as Universities Minister did establish a high-level stakeholder working group on Brexit, which included the President of the Royal Society, the chairs of the university mission groups and Universities UK amongst others (Department for Business, Energy and Industrial Strategy, 2017b). However, university leaders and lobby groups became sceptical as to the extent of the influence it wielded (Croft, 2017). In January 2017, as it was becoming increasingly clear that the scientific community in particular was failing to change the weather within government, an article in *Nature* called on the UK's scientists 'not to take this rout lying down' and to mount concerted political opposition to government policy (Macilwain, 2017, p. 6). The EU element of the republic of science was in jeopardy — but it was not yet lost.

UK RESEARCH IN A EUROPEAN CONTEXT

It is worth taking stock at this point of the relative position of UK research in a European context, and itemising the material benefits which UKRI gain through EU membership.

As has been discussed, the European Union is a major source of research funding for UK universities and research organisations. This funding emanates from a range of sources, including the Framework Programmes (the current iteration — FP8 — being known as Horizon 2020), the European Regional Development Fund (ERDF) and Euratom. Horizon 2020 has an estimated of €80bn, split between three pillars; 'Excellent Science', 'Industrial Leadership' and 'Societal Challenges' (European Commission, 2014b, pp. 7–15). Within the first pillar, 'Excellent Science', sits the European Research Council, founded in 2007 and with a budget of €13.095bn for the seven-year cycle of the programme (European Commission, 2014b, p. 7). Whilst Horizon — which through various mechanisms supports collaborative projects between industrial consortia and universities — has a clear emphasis on maximising the potential economic benefits of research — the remit of the ERC is drawn to enshrine academic independence. The key emphasis is on 'frontier research':

> Some of today's most significant inventions are the result of our natural curiosity about the way the world works. Although curiosity driven research at the frontiers of knowledge is rarely explicitly in support of commercial products, its discoveries nonetheless stimulate countless innovations. However, frontier research is often the first area to face cuts in times of economic difficulty, which is why through the ERC the EU is boosting the level of investment. Excellence is the sole criterion here for EU funding, which is awarded to individual researchers or research teams. (European Commission, 2014b, p. 7)

More than this, the EU represents a major vehicle for collaboration between scholars and scientists across its territorial range (and beyond). Advocates for UK research testifying to the post-referendum enquiries of the House of Commons and House of Lords' select committees made reference to the research 'ecosystem' (House of Lords Science and Technology Committee, 2016, p. 3), which is to say the whole research and knowledge transfer landscape. As Rob Davidson notes:

> It's not so much about the money, it's about the other things — the collaboration, the harmonisation, the ability to have specialised groups across the EU coming together — this division of labour that's been seen as a good thing since the 1800s [since] the end of mercantilism. (Davidson, 2017)

The Education Select Committee also cited collaboration as a key feature of UK higher education's interactions with the EU:

> Universities repeatedly placed continued participation in Horizon 2020 and successor programmes as a priority for the sector. Imperial College London expressed concern about the loss of EU research funding, calling the impact of its potential loss on universities' research productivity 'substantial', and that 'a simple pound-for-pound replacement of lost income would still be a net loss for science and research' due to the decline in collaboration. (House of Commons Education Committee, 2017, p. 18)

The benefits accruing to UK universities, research organisations and those working within them are anchored within the EU's freedoms — not least freedom of movement. The European Union includes well over 3300 higher education institutions, with whom — prior to Brexit — British scholars and scientists are free to collaborate without the hindrances of visa costs or immigration bureaucracy (European Commission, 2003) A Universities UK report in April 2017 showed that the scale of collaboration between UK researchers and their European counterparts is growing, with around half of UK research papers available through Web of Science published with an international co-author. This was up from just 5% of papers published in 1981 (Adams, 2017). The national share of co-authorship of papers with EU partners was 30.7% of all published research (Adams, 2017). The report also made a link to quality, and deeper collaboration at particular institutions:

> Collaboration is closely associated with exceptional performance. Collectively, UCL, Imperial, Oxford and Cambridge publish about one-quarter of the UK's research output. Their international collaboration has expanded more than the UK overall, to 57.7% of total publications in 2016 (compared to a 52.6% UK average: …) and their collaboration with the EU is 35.3% compared to 30.7%. (Adams, 2017)

But the money also matters. Britain's university system is a net beneficiary of EU grant income (Freeman, 2015; Royal Society, 2015, p. 3). This offsets a significant lack of spending at home; Britain spends the least of all G8 economies on research and development (Rohn, Curry, & Steele, 2015). In the austerity years, British higher education research funding was cut. As the LSE Commission on the Future of Britain in Europe noted, as a consequence UK receipts of EU research funding have soared:

> the small print shows that research income from the UK research councils took a knock after the

> financial crisis of 2008 and has not fully recovered.
> The EU has come to the rescue. Research income from
> the EU at €0.8bn (£0.5bn) in 2013-14 has risen by
> almost 170% since 2004-2005. (Corbett, 2016, p. 5)

This was a point reinforced by Ken Mayhew:

> letters in *Times Higher Education* (THE) claimed
> that almost three-quarters of the *increase* in higher
> education institution (HEI) science funding between
> 2007 and 2014 came from EU sources. (Mayhew,
> 2016, p. 158)

During the FP7 scheme of funding allocation (which predated Horizon 2020), UK universities, research organisations and industry received €6.9bn of funding through its provisions (Royal Society, 2015, p. 14). This amounted to 15.5% of the total funding available, ranking the United Kingdom second in terms of funding received and project participations (Universities UK, 2016c, p. 16). When the focus is narrowed specifically to institutions of higher and secondary education, excluding industrial partners and independent industrial projects, the figures become still more stark. UK universities and other educational institutions received over a quarter of all funds allocated to educational institutions; this amounted to a sum of €4.97bn (Universities UK, 2016c, p. 16). Four UK universities ranked among the top 10 in Europe for funding received, and the United Kingdom led the way in first place for funding received by educational institutions (Universities UK, 2016c, p. 16). The United Kingdom was receiving more from FP7 than its share of population or GDP merited, reflecting the underlying research strength and prestige of the UK university sector (Corbett, 2016, p. 19).

A report into EU support for UKRI, jointly commissioned by the Royal Society, the British Academy, the Academy of

Medical Sciences and the Royal Academy of Engineering, was published in May 2017. It drilled down into the 'granular' aspects of the relationship, and revealed the extent to which individual institutions and disciplines were dependent on EU support (Technopolis, 2017, p. 1). STEM research predictably garnered the largest sums — the top 10 disciplines ranked by scale of funding received were all STEM subjects. The President of the Royal Society, Venki Ramakrishnan, claimed that such 'EU funding sources are essential for UK science and innovation' (*Financial Times*, 2017).

But the sums involved only tell part of the story. As the report notes, whilst in absolute terms the sciences were the biggest beneficiaries, in relative terms EU funding can be more important to Arts, Humanities and Social Science disciplines (Technopolis, 2017, p. 16). In fact, Archaeology is the discipline most dependent on EU research funding, with 38% of its grant income originating with EU bodies (Technopolis, 2017, p. 16). Classics comes second, drawing 33% of its grant income from EU sources. Of the top ten disciplines by proportion of overall research income, only two are STEM subjects (IT and Chemistry, in third and tenth places, respectively) (Technopolis, 2017, p. 16). As the report puts it, 'the analysis suggests these subject areas [in the arts, humanities and social sciences] may be amongst the most at risk from any change in the terms of access to EU funds going forward' (Technopolis, 2017, p. 16). A spokesperson for the British Academy told the *Financial Times* that the 'high proportion of EU funding in these disciplines demonstrates the limited funding sources that exist within the UK' (*Financial Times*, 2017). The Director of the CRASSH, Professor Simon Goldhill, commented that:

> For the arts and humanities in particular [Brexit]
> will be totally disastrous, in the sense that all the

> new funding that is coming from the government,
> which is very, very large, which is focused on the
> Global Challenges Research Fund, is research that is
> designedly instrumental, and designedly aimed at
> ODA [Overseas Development Aid] compliant work.
> (Goldhill, 2017)

In the case of Classics this had serious potential consequences:

> [I]t's almost necessarily going to discount classics, or
> any form of classics research, or research into antiq-
> uity. So, the knock-on effects of both the cutting of
> the ERC plus the focus on the GCRF will mean dim-
> inution of potential research funds and activity in
> classics in the general sphere. And I think you can
> already see that happening … there's a lot of work
> going into the GCRF; what that requires is work
> that can show economic benefit for countries of low
> income. It's extremely hard if you're a classical phi-
> lologist to make your work look anything like that.
> (Goldhill, 2017)

Goldhill also emphasised the nature of ERC funding, which
was of longer duration than was typically the case with UK
government funding, allowing for the potential to build clusters and develop interdisciplinary teams 'which puts us
twenty years ahead of America in dealing with these issues'
(Goldhill, 2017). He echoed the views of the science lobby in
noting the vitality of international collaboration — 'no-one
university has the strength to deal with these problems'
(Goldhill, 2017). Moreover, these projects addressed tangible
social issues:

> I've been working on a project on how the secular
> university deals with religious diversity, which is a

> burning problem, for which the ... government has
> produced the Prevent strategy, which is hopeless, but
> actually if you want to understand the ways in
> which Christians, Jews and Muslims are interacting
> across the world, to take the three so-called
> Abrahamic faiths, you actually can't do that in one
> university ... we need to able to work with universi-
> ties in Germany and Israel and elsewhere to create
> the sort of understanding we need to approach that
> problem. (Goldhill, 2017)

The support offered by EU bodies applied not merely to this kind of collaboration in the arts and humanities but to the social sciences too. As the LSE Commission put it:

> The social sciences are another example where EU
> funding for cross-border work may be small scale
> but is critical to certain developments. There has
> been a reflexive response within the EU. The recent
> programmes integrate a social science strand into its
> big science and technology projects. (Corbett, 2016,
> p. 10)

The Technopolis report also drew attention to the regional distribution of funding. Whereas UK domestic research funding — both through the research councils and through quality-related HEFCE funding ('QR' funding) tends to be skewed towards the 'Golden Triangle' of Oxford, Cambridge and London, EU funding is more widely distributed. This is in part because, aside from Horizon funding, EU monies are also distributed through structural funds which have as a stated objective the economic development of relatively-disadvantaged regions (Technopolis, 2017, p. 28). Funding is also more distributed between types of institutions; although STEM-heavy large institutions from the Russell Group lead the way in terms of total sums gained, again as a proportion of income these institutions are less exposed than some other smaller and more specialist institutions.

Goldsmith's College, University of London, drew 61% of its total research income from EU sources in the 2014/2015 academic year (Technopolis, 2017, p. 17). The top 10 institutions most exposed to a potential loss of EU research funding were geographically disparate — from the University of South Wales (41% of research funding drawn from the EU) to Bangor University (38%) and Sheffield Hallam University (35%) (Technopolis, 2017, p. 17). Sheffield Hallam did not take an official position during the EU referendum, but its vice-chancellor, Chris Husbands — the incoming chair of the TEF — noted that the United Kingdom as whole did 'extremely well out of EU research funding' (Husbands, British Universities and Brexit, 2016).

The successor programme, Horizon 2020, is still ongoing, but the United Kingdom has continued to punch above its weight in terms of population and the size of the economy. Tables 1–5, adapted from an official UK government release in February 2017 (Department for Business, Energy and Industrial Strategy, 2017a), give a sense of the extent to which UK higher education is benefiting from access to European research funding.

Some of this funding was derived from Euratom (Hinson, 2017). Euratom was established in 1957 at the same time as the EEC, and the United Kingdom joined in 1973 at the same time as joining the EEC (Hinson, 2017, p. 3). Euratom funds research in nuclear physics, notably into nuclear fusion, and is a major funder of the Culham Centre for Fusion Energy in Oxfordshire (House of Lords Science and Technology Committee, 2016, p. 58). It provides a regulatory framework for the inspection of nuclear materials (derived in large part from the stipulations of the International Atomic Energy Authority), and a common nuclear market for materials and

Table 1. Top 10 Subject Areas by Amount of EU Funding in 2014/2015.

HESA Cost Centre	EU Government Bodies Income in 2014/2015 (in £)
101 Clinical medicine	119,913,000
112 Biosciences	90,766,000
114 Physics	55,403,000
113 Chemistry	54,558,000
121 IT, systems sciences and computer software engineering	46,208,000
119 Electrical, electronic and computer engineering	39,290,000
120 Mechanical, aero and production engineering	34,633,000
111 Earth, marine and environmental sciences	34,538,000
115 General engineering	28,116,000
122 Mathematics	18,982,000

Source: Adapted from Technopolis (2017, p. 17).

staff within its signatory states (House of Commons Business, Energy and Industrial Strategy Committee, 2017, p. 28). Switzerland, a non-EU state, is an associate member (Hinson, 2017, p. 7). Under the provisions of Euratom, the United Kingdom is able to source nuclear fuel and other materials from other states within the treaty, in addition to engaging in collaboration, in particular on fusion energy research (House of Commons Business, Energy and Industrial Strategy Committee, 2017, p. 33). The Joint European Torus is a collaborative endeavour based at Culham, and is what is

Table 2. Top 10 Higher Education Institutions by Amount of EU Funding in 2014/2015.

Higher Education Institution	Income from EU Government Bodies in 2014/2015 (in £)
The University of Oxford	60,280,000
The University of Cambridge	59,495,000
University College London	45,710,000
Imperial College of Science, Technology and Medicine	41,929,000
The University of Edinburgh	25,680,000
King's College London	24,845,000
The University of Manchester	23,741,000
The University of Sheffield	20,414,000
The University of Bristol	18,623,000
The University of Leeds	18,191,000

Source: Adapted from Technopolis (2017, p. 19).

known as a 'tokamak' — 'a magnetic fusion device designed to prove the feasibility of fusion as a large-scale and carbon-free source of energy' (Hinson, Euratom, 2017, p. 11). It is a precursor to the forthcoming International Thermonuclear Experimental Reactor, which is being constructed in France and in which — through Euratom — the UK is playing a significant role (House of Lords Science and Technology Committee, 2016, p. 58). Finally, in this non-exhaustive list of Euratom's functions, the treaty and the community it constitutes also regulate the transfer of medical isotopes (Hinson, 2017, p. 9).

Euratom is not part of the EU, constituted as it is by a separate treaty. However, it is linked to it — with Euratom's

Table 3. UK Participations in Horizon 2020.

Participations	Total Participations	UK Participations	UK Share of Total Participations (%)	EU 28 Participations	UK Share of EU 28 Participations (%)	UK Ranking (Share of Total Participations)
Total excluding Euratom	50,111	6459	12.9	45,637	14.2	1st
Total including Euratom	50,528	6485	12.8	46,024	14.1	1st
EC Funding	**EC Total Funding (€ Millions)**	**EC Funding to the UK (€ Millions)**	**UK Share of EC Total Funding (%)**	**EC Funding to EU 28 (€ Millions)**	**UK share of EC Funding to EU 28 (%)**	**UK Ranking (Share of Total EC Funding)**
Total excluding Euratom	20,649	3234	15.7	19,188	16.9	2nd
Total including Euratom	21,164	3266	15.4	19,697	16.6	2nd

Source: Adapted from Department for Business, Energy and Industrial Strategy (2017a).

Table 4. UK HEIs' Participations in Horizon 2020.

Type	Total	UK	UK Share (%)	EU 28 Participations	UK Share of EU 28 Participations (%)	UK Ranking
Higher or secondary education establishments	16,639	3720	22.4	14,846	25.1	1st

Source: Adapted from Department for Business, Energy and Industrial Strategy (2017a).

provisions being subject to the remit of the ECJ. And, as the Business, Energy and Industrial Select Committee put it, this last provision made it 'politically unfeasible' that the United Kingdom could remain in Euratom given the 'government's objective to leave the European Court of Justice' (House of Commons Business, Energy and Industrial Strategy Committee, 2017, p. 29). This then is the reason why, in March 2017, Prime Minister Theresa May gave notice of the UK's withdrawal from Euratom under the provisions of Article 106a of the Euratom treaty (d'Urso, 2017). May had made withdrawing from the jurisdiction of the ECJ a centrepiece of her approach to Brexit; her decision to withdraw was, however, highly contentious. Professor Steven Cowley, the former head of the Culham centre and the UK Atomic Energy Authority, described it as 'bonkers' (Else, 2017b). The BEIS Select Committee expressed fears that withdrawal from Euratom would leave the United Kingdom with insufficient time to establish an inspections regime to International Atomic Energy Authority (IAEA) standards, given that this work was currently undertaken by Euratom (House of Commons Business, Energy

Table 5. Top 30 UK HEIs by Receipt of Horizon Funding.

Organisation Name	Total Participations	EC Funding (ϵ)	Ranking (Share of EC Funding to All HES[a] Organisations)
University of Oxford	267	186,087,964	1st
University of Cambridge	285	179,926,792	2nd
University College London	249	172,404,776	3rd
Imperial College London	198	127,662,205	4th
The University of Edinburgh	145	104,373,087	8th
The University of Manchester	123	75,224,479	10th
London School of Hygiene and Tropical Medicine	19	70,580,607	13th
University of Southampton	83	63,297,290	20th
University of Bristol	103	61,198,164	24th
University of Birmingham	118	52,909,457	33th
University of Warwick	85	51,593,638	36th
University of Sheffield	107	50,397,361	39th
University of Glasgow	88	48,270,710	41st
King's College London	79	45,645,379	45th
University of Exeter	67	44,264,963	46th
University of Leeds	84	39,483,245	48th
University of Newcastle upon Tyne	83	36,156,880	54th
University of Nottingham	83	34,551,755	60th
London School of Economics and Political Science	43	27,387,019	74th
Queen Mary University of London	63	26,844,229	79th

Table 5. (*Continued*)

Organisation Name	Total Participations	EC Funding (€)	Ranking (Share of EC Funding to All HES[a] Organisations)
Cardiff University	50	25,950,905	81st
University of York	52	25,475,715	84th
University of Liverpool	53	24,251,984	88th
University of Bath	34	22,661,179	100th
Queen's University of Belfast	51	20,719,216	107th
University of Durham	42	20,202,885	108th
University of Strathclyde	58	20,010,028	112th
University of St Andrews	36	19,887,806	115th
University of Sussex	34	17,926,999	124th
University of Reading	30	17,305,758	128th

Source: Adapted from Department for Business, Energy and Industrial Strategy (2017a).
Note: [a]The Horizon category is officially 'Higher and Secondary Education'.

and Industrial Strategy Committee, 2017, pp. 30–31). Indeed, the Select Committee noted in its report that 'the scale and number of British nuclear facilities mean that a quarter of all Euratom staff time dedicated to safeguards is spent in the UK' (House of Commons Business, Energy and Industrial Strategy Committee, 2017, p. 31). For universities, and research more generally, the dangers involved in leaving Euratom are profound, as the select committee notes:

> Exclusion from Euratom's research programmes
> could disadvantage national nuclear research, limit

the UK's future access to global developments in
fusion, and reduce the substantial business opportunities for UK firms supplying Euratom research
projects. (House of Commons Business, Energy and
Industrial Strategy Committee, 2017, p. 33)

But, profoundly concerning as that is, Euratom touched a
nerve in the media in a way other aspects of Britain's research
networks didn't. This was because it regulates the transfer
of medical isotopes used in scans for cancer patients.
Figures quoted by the Royal College of Radiologists suggested 10,000 patients were at risk if the UK were to leave
Euratom without alternative arrangements in place (Merrick,
2017).

Finally, Euratom highlights another aspect of the UK's
participation in European research networks which is of real
concern — the issue of regulation. At time of writing, the EU
is in the process of introducing a new directive on data protection (Royal Society, 2015, p. 18). At present, UK-based
researchers are able to transfer data to EU27-based researchers knowing that the respective legal regimes for handling
that data are — under the aegis of EU law — mutually-
compliant. Moreover, as the Royal Society (2015, p. 18) and
the Wellcome Trust (2017) have both noted , safeguards for
the transfer of research data were only agreed after extensive
lobbying by the UK research community, influence which will
be lost once the UK ceases to be a member state. If the UK
continues on its course of a 'hard Brexit', unless it implements
all subsequent European regulatory law, it may prove impossible for certain cross-border research to take place. This is
only on the grounds of data protection. As we have seen with
Euratom, there are many other potential points of fracture.

EU funding and its associated research networks are
invaluable to UK higher education. The funding provides

support to develop clusters of researchers, the purchase of infrastructure including expensive equipment and allows for a greater distribution of funding beyond the 'golden triangle' than has proved possible with UK domestic funding sources. Moreover, the EU's commitment to academic peer review, and the determination to support 'frontier research' in the long-term, presents research funding of a significantly dissimilar character to that provided by UK state agencies.

Neither the sector nor government was unaware of the scale of the EU's investment in British higher education research — or, in turn, the sector's investment in the EU. But the divide between the opposing views of Brexit's implications for higher education and research in the build-up to the EU referendum were well-summarised by an LSE Commission on the Future of Britain and Europe report:

> 'Remain' reflects the sector's concerns, 'leave' sets out to appeal to those who want the big picture, not the detail. The sector's strength lies in its tried and trusted experience of European cooperation. It has attracted top level political support (103 vice chancellors, 15 past and present ministers for universities and science, 15 past and present presidents of the National Union of Students, more than 60,000 scientists, and the House of Lords Science and Technology Committee). (Corbett, 2016, p. 5)

In similar vein to rhetorical debates over British exports to the EU more generally, British higher education was characterised by Leave supporters as 'exceptional', playing on the British exceptionalism discourse at the heart of Leave rhetoric (Finn M., 2016b). Conceived of as a world leader independent of the EU, British higher education would 'get a deal' with the EU purely because it was in that organisation's interests to make such an agreement happen. This was wilfully naïve, and assumed a UK government negotiating posture towards the EU which was not forthcoming. The alternative argument — that the UK could simply fund its own research with monies saved from its contribution to the EU budget, also denied the insight offered by Imperial College — that, due to the collaborative nature of EU funding, even 'a pound for pound replacement' of funding would still represent 'a net loss for science and research' (House of Commons Education Committee, 2017, p. 18). This is not to mention the divergent character of the EU's approach to research support when contrasted with the UK government's, an issue we shall turn to next.

THE NATIONALISATION OF UKRI

In December 2014, the UK government — then a Conservative-Liberal Democrat coalition — published *Our Plan for Growth*, its new 'science and innovation strategy' (Department for Business, Innovation and Skills, 2014). This was co-signed by the Chancellor of the Exchequer, George Osborne, the Business Secretary, Vince Cable, and the minister for universities and science, Greg Clark (Department for Business, Innovation and Skills, 2014, p. 4) This placed science at the 'heart' of the coalition government's much-vaunted 'long-term economic plan' (Department for Business, Innovation and Skills, 2014, p. 5). A key emphasis was 'commercialisation', with the government 'recognis[ing] the vital role that commercialisation of science and new technologies play in our future growth', and lamenting that 'UK innovation is still seen internationally as excellent in science but weak in commercialisation' (Department for Business, Innovation and Skills, 2014, pp. 3, 69).

As part of the strategy, the government commissioned a review of the academic research councils charged with disbursing research funding to the UK academic research community (Department for Business, Innovation and Skills, 2014, p. 7). Authored by the former President of the Royal Society Sir Paul Nurse, an eminent geneticist Nobel laureate in medicine, it was published in December 2015 (Nurse, 2015). Nurse argued for the creation of a new body to superintend the Research Councils. Nurse called this body Research UK, and it would supersede the existing Research Councils UK with a view to driving forward 'strategic' research priorities and 'cross-cutting' work. This would be achieved, in part, with better 'co-ordination' with bodies including Innovate UK and 'commercial and philanthropic research, as far as is possible' (Nurse, 2015, p. 26) The chief executive 'should be a highly distinguished scientist' (Nurse, 2015, p. 27).

Though Nurse aimed to be inclusive in his definition of 'science' (Nurse, 2015, p. 2), the discussion around the review further marginalised the arts and humanities, and to some extent the social sciences. Though Nurse's vision for research was regarded by some as an attempt to preserve the role and autonomy of the Research Councils, this was against the grain of government policy, and when effect was given to Nurse's recommendations as part of the white paper preceding the Higher Education and Research Bill, *Success as a Knowledge Economy* (Department for Business, Innovation and Skills, 2016b), they were modified. Research UK gave way to a more powerful body, UKRI, which would include Innovate UK, and 'ensure that our research and innovation system is sufficiently strategic and agile to deliver national capability for the future that drives discovery and growth' (Department for Business, Innovation and Skills, 2016a, p. 20). It would 'incorporate the functions of the seven

Research Councils, Innovate UK, and HEFCE's research funding functions. The names and brands of the Research Councils and Innovate UK will be retained' (Department for Business, Innovation and Skills, 2016a, p. 20). Most significant appeared to the curbs on academic autonomy and the drive towards a government role in setting the direction of academic research:

> UKRI will have a strong board with responsibility
> for leading on overall strategic direction, cross-
> cutting decision making and advising the Secretary
> of State on the balance of funding between research
> disciplines. The board will manage funds with cross-
> disciplinary impact and a 'common research fund'
> as proposed by Paul Nurse. There would be a
> legislative requirement for the Secretary of State
> to consider the need for both academic and
> business representation and expertise on the Board.
> (Department for Business, Innovation and Skills,
> 2016a, p. 20)

Though the government was quick to 'restate' its 'commitment to the Haldane Principle' (Department for Business, Innovation and Skills, 2016a, p. 20), sector figures were wary. The Haldane Principle is the commitment by government that the direction of research and thence the spending of research funding is a matter reserved to academics, and dates back to a series of reports chaired by Lord Haldane as the universities' support mechanisms were developed in the early 20th century (Hughes, 2011). In short, the Haldane Principle enshrines a central facet of academic autonomy — that they alone should determine what should be researched. But it is a feature of the UK university landscape that has been under considerable pressure for many years. Financial crises feature prominently in assaults on university autonomy; in 1946 the Attlee Government considered changes in the machinery of government to subordinate universities to the fulfilment of 'national needs'[1]. In the wake of the 2008 financial crisis, and in the era of the 'knowledge economy' discourse, universities and their research were seen as potential magic bullets to restore the UK to growth, albeit ones that would require 'strategic' management (Hughes, 2011). In the words of Alan Hughes:

> In the UK, during the course of 2008 and 2009, a series of policy announcements and speeches by ministers at the then Department of Innovation, Universities and Skills stressed the importance of universities in the development of innovative strategies to recover from the recession. In doing so, the need for a strategic allocation of research resources was emphasised, in terms of both the restructuring of the economy in the aftermath of the collapse of financial services and of the perceived need to redevelop strengths in manufacturing activities. This was contemporaneous with a renewed emphasis on identifying and measuring the effect of publicly-funded research and changes which required applicants to the UK research councils to provide an indication of the wider 'impact' of their proposed research.
> (Hughes, 2011, p. 412)

In this light, the development of UKRI was a continuation of a policy trend, one which sought ostensibly to address the 'concern in the UK with weaknesses in the links between research carried out in universities and its commercialisation' (Hughes, 2011, p. 416). The business case for UKRI stated that 'one of Innovate UK's priorities'

is to turn scientific excellence into economic impact,
and deliver results through innovation, in collaboration with the research community. It works
closely with the research councils to identify ways
co-operation can be increased. Integration of the
bodies will help simplify and streamline co-operation
to the benefit of both communities. (Department for
Business, Innovation and Skills, 2016a, p. 8)

The creation of the new body would

result in improved collaboration between the
research base and the commercialisation of discoveries in the business community, thereby ensuring that
research outcomes can be fully exploited for the benefit of the UK. (Department for Business, Innovation
and Skills, 2016a, p. 27)

Alongside UKRI was another intervention into UK research
priorities, namely the establishment of the Global Challenges
Research Fund (GCRF). This fund, announced in the 2015
Spending Review, allocated £1.5bn of funding towards projects that could contribute to the UK's contributions to overseas aid. Notwithstanding the status of the British Academy
as a 'delivery partner', this was a Fund which prioritised
science (Department for Business, Energy and Industrial
Strategy, 2017c, p. 3). Moreover, in its emphasis on 'cross-
cutting' and 'strategy', the 'delivery partners' were to be
prodded by the ODA board, chaired by the universities
minister, who would hold 'delivery partners' to account
(Department for Business, Energy and Industrial Strategy,
2017a, p. 10). Ominously, one of the concerns government
had for the future efficacy of the GCRF was the potential
for lack of 'buy-in from the communities which need to be
mobilised to realise its ambitions, including researchers and

non-academic partners in the UK …' (Department for Business, Energy and Industrial Strategy, 2017c, p. 8). The tighter governance arrangements were intended to prevent that from happening.

For its part, the Higher Education and Research Bill was introduced in the Commons by the Education Secretary Justine Greening a little more than a month before the EU referendum. Within it were provisions to establish UKRI, the Office for Students ('a new all-powerful regulator for universities' according to the *Times Higher Education* magazine) (Grove, 2016) and to introduce the TEF, a new audit exercise which was intended to offer an official assessment of teaching to parallel the existing REF (Higher Education Funding Council for England, 2017). Taken together, it amounted to the biggest change in university governance in nearly 25 years (Morris D., 2017b). The broader implications of this are addressed in the next chapter.

After the Brexit decision, this determination to redraw the whole higher education landscape drew fire. Gordon Marsden, the shadow higher education minister (Grove, 2016), Sally Hunt, the General Secretary of the Universities and Colleges Union (UCU) (*The Guardian*, 2016a), David Phoenix, Vice-Chancellor of London South Bank University (Grove, 2016), Stuart Croft, Vice-Chancellor of the University of Warwick (Coventry Observer, 2016) and *The Guardian* newspaper (*The Guardian*, 2016b), in a powerful editorial, all called for the government to either delay or withdraw the legislation. *The Guardian* put it succinctly — universities were 'facing a double whammy':

> [I]n years to come, 2016 may look like the high point before the decline: the consequences of Brexit, a slump in the number of 18-year-olds and, above all, a misconceived higher education bill, will all

> take their toll ... 14% of universities' research
> funding comes from EU programmes — much more
> in some faculties — often forming the basis for
> important research partnerships ... It also reinvents
> arrangements for research funding, amalgamating
> all nine existing research councils into a single entity,
> UK Research and Innovation. The bill was conceived
> when few imagined the Brexit vote would be lost,
> plunging universities into an unknown future. The
> government should pause. This is no time to upend
> one of our most successful exports. (*The Guardian*,
> 2016b)

Others called it a 'perfect storm':

> The 'perfect storm' is a word that I've been using, as
> well as the 'marginal losses' analogy ... The perfect
> storm is a thing ... the way science has been going
> internationally is that you have open science, open
> data ... But instead the UK's plan seems to be go
> more towards the American model. And America's
> been quite good at open data, but it does have this
> model where the really good universities have patent
> offices and they wrap up their knowledge and then
> they make money out of it. And that seems to be the
> long-term economic plan of Osborne and Theresa
> May, and it's not changed because of Brexit.
> (Davidson, 2017)

One vice-chancellor claimed that, despite Brexit, in terms of
its reforms the government had simply 'carried on regardless'
(Croft, 2017). The Education Select Committee noted that
the 'wide-ranging Bill creates extra uncertainty for the sector
during Brexit negotiations' (House of Commons Education
Committee, 2017, p. 5). Jo Johnson, for his part, upbraided

university leaders who had called for a pause in his subsequent speech to Universities UK, characterising them as those 'relatively few voices out there calling for a Brexit-related delay' (Johnson, 2016a).

The Government's draft *Industrial and Innovation Strategy* was published in January 2017. UKRI was central to its ambitions; UKRI would 'develop and deliver a clear strategy from fundamental research through to business innovation' (Department for Business, Energy and Industrial Strategy, 2017d, p. 29). It reiterated the government's priorities in relation to 'commercialisation', bemoaning the fact that UK universities 'register far fewer patents' than US ones (Department for Business, Energy and Industrial Strategy, 2017d, p. 27). As Davidson notes, it also highlighted the Regional Partnerships Investment Fund (RPIF), where business consortia led by universities could engage in 'capital infrastructure' development (Department for Business, Energy and Industrial Strategy, 2017d, p. 29). But the downside from a higher education point of view was the draft strategy's contention that there had to be an alternative funding stream where universities were not involved. Davidson claims that:

> If you look at how they're going to spend the money
> often it is about sidelining higher education and
> focusing on the industrial sector … The problem
> [with the RPIF for them] is that it has a university
> involved; 'we want to recreate this fund but we
> want to remove the need for a university to be there'
> [is the government's view]. (Davidson, 2017)

Whilst scientists feared that the government's approach to science and innovation in the post-Brexit era would centre on commercialisation to the exclusion of all else, academics in the arts and humanities found it difficult to see where their research fitted within the new landscape. The Cambridge classicist Robin Osborne sat on the British Academy's research and higher education policy committee until 2017. From that vantage point he remarked that

> There is no doubt in the minds of those in the Academy who have to engage with BEIS, as it now is, that attitudes there have hardened, that the agenda has got ever-more biased towards STEM, and that actually government policy is very much being determined by middle[-ranking] civil servants who have seen themselves as having a sort of mission to push the STEM side of things, and so I think the climate has changed there, for the worse for arts and humanities. (Osborne, 2017)

CONCLUSION

The United Kingdom stands to lose a great deal in terms of funding and collaborative opportunities in research as a consequence of the Brexit decision. In the first of these two categories we can see a clear and unambiguous 'economic' implication. But, in research terms, the significance of the Brexit moment for UK higher education is greater even than that. Politically, the Brexit moment is likely to accelerate trends of centralisation of research, and taken together with the reforms to teaching audit and university regulation discussed in Chapters two and four, this will have major consequences for the very essence of higher education in the United Kingdom. Culturally, the area of research, or scholarship, is one where academic citizens define themselves as academics, and not, say, teachers; research — or put more broadly, the 'advancement of knowledge' — is the fundamental raison *d'etre* of the university (Truscot, 1944). It may be the singular activity which differentiates it from a school. And the undertaking of research enshrines norms of intellectual exchange and conduct which are, in fact, borderless. UK government policy both before and since the 2016 referendum on membership of the European Union has been inimical to these norms of academic citizenship. The language of UK government documents on research and innovation in Brexit Britain is emphatically nationalistic, rejecting the claims of a republic of science (not to mention the scholarly realm of the arts and humanities) in favour of a commodification of domestic UK innovation. As such, it fundamentally misconceives the nature of research and academic inquiry in the service of political objectives. It betrays a 'culture of suspicion', to borrow Onora O'Neill's phrase (O'Neill, 2002), amongst policymakers, oriented towards academics who are seen as a producer interest. This is but part of a broader assault on expertise in public life which has consequences for the very health of democracy in the Brexit moment.

NOTE

1. See Chapter One.

PART II

THE IMPLICATIONS OF THE BREXIT MOMENT

CHAPTER FOUR

UNIVERSITIES AND SOCIETY IN MODERN BRITAIN

It isn't only rulers and governments that prize and need trust. Each and every profession and every institution needs trust.

— Baroness O'Neill of Bengarve,
Philosopher (2002).

I think people in this country have had enough of experts from organisations with acronyms saying that they know what is best for them and getting it consistently wrong.

— The Rt. Hon. Michael Gove MP,
former Secretary of State for Education and
Vote Leave campaigner, interview with Faisal Islam,
Sky News, 3 June 2016.

Thank you for your message. I am currently receiving an exceptionally high volume of emails and there may be a delay in replying to you.

*Sincere apologies if I do not manage to reply individ-
ually to the many thousands of messages I have
received from my fellow citizens, including those
now deeply concerned about the outcome of the
referendum and its implications for themselves, their
families and their country.*

*If you have sent me an abusive message, e.g. falsely
claiming that I am paid by the European
Commission / that I have my snout in the EU
trough / that I am only worried about saving my
own job / that you hope I get deported sooner rather
than later, please do not be offended if I do not treat
replying to your message as a priority.*

*If you have sent me a threatening email, or one con-
taining racist abuse, I will report it to the police.*

— Professor Michael Dougan, Professor of Law and
Jean Monnet Chair of European Law,
University of Liverpool, Email autoreply message,
June 2016.

UNIVERSITIES IN THE BREXIT MOMENT: A CRISIS
OF TRUST

In September 2017, a 'right of centre think tank' (Burns,
2017) named UK2020 published a report on Britain's universities. It was entitled *Timebomb: How the university cartel is
failing Britain's students* (Tice & Al-Humaidhi, 2017).
Co-written by the co-founder of LEAVE.EU, the property
developer Richard Tice, it was endorsed by Lord Adonis, the
former schools minister and Downing Street Head of Policy

who had helped reintroduce tuition fees under New Labour, and Sir Anthony Seldon, the Vice-Chancellor of the University of Buckingham, a private university which offers two-year degrees as part of its business model (Burns, 2017). The report was, in some ways, the perfect confluence of Brexit and the nostrums of neoliberal higher education policy. Tice was a prominent Brexiteer, as was Owen Paterson, chairman of the UK2020 think tank. UK2020 had previously published a report attacking the NHS, sponsored by a private medical diagnostics company and written by Kristian Niemietz of the free-market think tank, Institute of Economic Affairs (IEA) (Niemietz, 2016). Post-Brexit, Paterson, the former Environment Secretary, had been trumpeting the vote as a 'once in a lifetime opportunity' to deregulate sectors from agriculture to fisheries (Rayner & Hope, 2017). Seldon and Adonis for their part were iconoclasts. Following Seldon's arrival as Vice-Chancellor of the University of Buckingham in 2015, he had engaged in a series of broadsides against what he saw as the higher education sector's 'antiquated provision' (Burns, 2017). Having previously described higher education as a 'rotten deal' for students (Seldon, 2015), he commented in his foreword to the UK2020 report that:

> Universities are still run predominantly by academics and administrators for academics and administrators. The producer interest reigns. The voice of the consumer, in other words the student, has not been taken greatly into consideration …. (Seldon, 2017, p. 7)

The word 'cartel' in the report's subtitle (and with which the report was trailed) referred to Tice's allegation that the universities were (effectively) engaged in rigging the system in favour of high fees and high salaries for vice-chancellors, at the expense of students (Burns, 2017).

The publication of the report, and the attendant media furore, followed a summer when universities had been constantly under attack in the media, not least because of Adonis' interventions on the social network Twitter, where he routinely decried vice-chancellors for their salaries, and academics for their supposed-'three-month holiday' (Parr, 2017). Jim Dickinson, the Chief Executive of the University of East Anglia Students' Union, commented on the website WonkHE that VC salaries — 'despite the data being available for some years' amounted to a 'dirty little secret' at the heart of British higher education (Dickinson, 2017).

Except, whilst this was a useful fiction for the political purposes of some, the salaries weren't a secret of any kind whatsoever, dirty, little or otherwise. And despite the attempts of Seldon, Adonis and others to conflate academics and their VCs, the most trenchant criticism of spiralling VC pay had emanated from academics and trade unions. The present author, writing in 2015, commented that:

> Unsurprisingly for a sector now being run on market
> lines and undergoing a process of privatisation, uni-
> versity vice-chancellors increasingly cut themselves
> off from those they referred to as colleagues and
> ceased to be the chief custodians of scholarly guilds
> and instead became chief executives of, in many
> cases, very large businesses. The consequences were
> similar to those seen in other privatised concerns,
> and the avarice of vice-chancellors was comparable
> in kind (if not in degree) to that of the much-
> maligned investment bankers. The basic salary of
> a Russell Group vice-chancellor stood in 2014 at
> 'nearly 293,000 ... [with] pension contributions
> that goes up to £318,500'. At the same time,
> vice-chancellors asked academic staff to consider

> a real-terms pay cut ... and began to reconsider
> the viability of one of the major university pension
> schemes, all on the grounds of affordability.
> (Finn M., 2015c, pp. 93–94)

Though this particular passage of prose may well have gone unnoticed, the media coverage it drew on couldn't have. VC salaries were a regular bone of contention with the academics' union, UCU, and made the headlines repeatedly in the years after the Browne Review (Coughlan, 2015; Sellgren, 2016); in 2014 they had even been branded 'academic fat cats' by *The Independent* newspaper (Garner, 2014). Secret this was not.

What took place in the summer of 2017 — 'a terrible two months for universities in the news' as WonkHE dubbed it (Morris D., 2017c) — was a discursive framing of British universities characteristic of the tenets of neoliberal political economy. Universities were a 'cartel'. Students were 'sold a lie' (Burns, 2017). Academics were lazy and over-privileged, the beneficiaries of three-month vacations, or, in Seldon's words, 'wide open spaces of time when academics are writing and students are left to their own devices' (Seldon, 2017, p. 7). Taken at face value, this amounted to a 'crisis'. Seldon's views reflected those of the universities minister, Jo Johnson, who had repeatedly attacked universities' supposed lack of interest in pedagogy, had commented on 'mediocre teaching' and 'patchiness' in some parts of the sector (Johnson, 2016b). To remedy this, he had sponsored the introduction of a TEF audit mechanism, which paralleled the REF for scholarship and research (Higher Education Funding Council for England, 2017), which ostensibly would help further develop market pressures in higher education by providing more accurate information to students, driving up quality.

This 'policy trajectory' (Ball S., 1993) predated the Brexit moment, which brought its own crises to the university. The first and most immediate perhaps are the material crises outlined in the previous two chapters. But another was the broader crisis intimated in the opening chapter — that of an emergent, and newly recognised, gulf between university and society in Britain, a consistent enough presence to be considered a nationwide phenomenon, but one which had specific local contexts. All these crises can be interrogated through an overarching crisis — a crisis of trust. In the Brexit moment, Britain's universities aren't trusted by policymakers to teach and research well, or by the public to deliver expertise. This crisis of trust represents a real and fundamental 'crisis of academic authority' (Lybeck, 2018), which has its roots in a number of places and processes which this chapter will outline. At its most basic, this has its origins in the rapid transformation of UK higher education in the age of 'the great university gamble', and the unresolved question at the heart of it all — that of what universities are for (Collini, 2012).

CRISIS AND ITS USES

In policy discourse, fictive 'crises' are valuable, as they permit the dynamic remaking of the institutions framed by them (Ball S. J., 2008), and nowhere is this more true than in British higher education (Finn M., 2018a, 2018b), which has been in a 'never ending' series of crises since the end of the Second World War (at least). This parallels the growing role of the state and the market in creating and steering a set of institutions which, at a philosophical level, prize their 'autonomy'. The crises of expansion, funding, 'national needs' and — now — trust, allow for the insertion of outside forces to remake the institutions and their missions in service of other objectives. In the Brexit moment, such crises are both apparent and real. It does not betray too much of what follows to note that some of the 'crisis' of trust denoted above is rooted very much in the realm of the 'apparent' rather than the 'real', but in a world where perception is critical, it is possible for one to elide into the other. In fact, whilst some of the politically motivated premises of the present 'crisis' of trust are flat wrong, and in some cases wilfully so, they are discursively sustainable because they appeal to a regime of truth that has currency — the neoliberal vision of bloated, self-interested, producer groups, yes, but also the gulf of perception and understanding between universities and broader society in an age of marketisation. Such has been the rapidity of change in the higher education sector that 18-year olds who entered university in 2017 are the first students whose parents could reasonably have anticipated their children would have to pay fees when they elected to have them. The culture of the 'college fund' is absent in the United Kingdom — although the 'bank of mum and dad' is very real — and a 'moral economy' of free higher education still persists.

Neoliberal arguments also cut through for another reason — precisely because universities, their leaders, and — at times — their academic staff, have been far too keen to play the game and internalise the 'logic of competition' (Davies W., 2017) intrinsic to this 'moral-economic system' (Davies W., 2017, p. xviii) — in short, to accept the premise that the function of the university is fundamentally economic, and by extension that students are consumers and expertise is valuable insofar as it has (literal) currency, often exhibited through spin-out companies, patents or 'impact'. This showed itself to some degree in the Brexit debate itself, when universities were often slow to characterise the impact of Brexit in anything other than economic terms. This threw into relief the extent to which university administrations had themselves internalised the 'logic of competition' and, furthermore, reconceived their answer to the question 'what are universities for?' exclusively in terms of supporting the economy and 'delivering' for consumers.

As Frank Furedi notes, academia by its nature is an uneasy tension between competition — succeeding in one's field — and collaboration — acting as part of a scholarly community (Furedi, 2010). *Homo academicus*, as Pierre Borudieu described it, likes prizes and recognition (Bourdieu, 1988). It is a species designed for league tables and rankings. Internalising the broader logic of the university as a competitive business, and individual academics as 'entreprencurs' left universities vulnerable in the Brexit moment — when too often it seemed as though universities had lost any sense of what made them different from businesses, and thus unable to argue their case as other than a 'vested interest' on Brexit, or even on matters relating to their own teaching and research practices.

Indeed, the rapid evolution of mass higher education in the United Kingdom since 1992 — and the even-more rapid evolution of the fees regime since 1998 — has placed the university and its academics not merely as victims of the Brexit moment in British political culture, but, at least in some small part, culpable in its arrival. Neoliberalism is a term ubiquitous in scholarship on higher education in the past decade. In Will Davies' words, neoliberalism is both 'the elevation of market-based principles and techniques of evaluation to the level of state-endorsed norms' and, more fundamentally, 'the disenchantment of politics by economics' (Davies W., 2017, p. xiv). Davies elaborates on the simple elision of neoliberalism and 'market fundamentalism'. It is also about the repurposing of other, ostensibly 'non-economic' fields through the 'principle' and 'logic' of values such as 'competition'. Davies specifies universities as one such institution reformed and repurposed, where the logic of competition has become entrenched and where market-based values now predominate. For Furedi, this is emblematised in the transformation of the student into a consumer, where the consumer wants and desires of the student and their 'pushy parent' 'discipline' the academic, who is now conceived of merely as a service provider. And for John Smyth (Smyth, 2017), echoing Davies, the tragedy of it all is that neoliberalism is in practice 'dead' as a convincing rationale for political action, with universities slavishly adhering to a 'zombie' paradigm and conniving in the dissolution of their own authority. Neoliberalism's (such as it was) legitimacy died in 2008; yet nothing has replaced it. Instead, its norms of consumption-driven growth remain, and the remoulding of academic institutions in this vein continues.

Within the higher education reform literature, policies, such as the introduction of tuition fees, the rise of audit, and the development of the (marketable) concept of the 'student experience', have all been grouped under the heading of 'neoliberalism'. Some (situated) authors reject this as 'hyperbole' (Hillman, 2016), but — though it is too-often used in education policy studies as an explanatory catch-all — neoliberalism is real. It is a governmentality of policymaking which is based on a vernacular understanding of economic theory. Whilst Davies and others trace the intellectual lineage of neoliberalism to Hayek and von Mises through the Chicago School and beyond (Davies W., 2017; Stedman Jones, 2012) — and there is a growing literature on the history of neoliberalism in the UK (Jackson, 2010; Sutcliffe-Braithwaite, 2012) — the criticism of its use as a concept in practice often arises from the perceived ahistorical nature of such usages. There is some merit to this criticism. Although as David Harvey chronicles there are common threads to the ascent of

neoliberalism and free-market values in Western political culture (Harvey, 2005), such triumphs as these values have
enjoyed are still mediated by the particularity of place and
time, and should not be blithely deterritorialised. Though
Smyth and Giroux may see neoliberalism's impact on higher
education as universal in nature, it is untrue to say that British
neoliberalism — 'really existing neoliberalism' (Davies W.,
2017) is the same as its American or Antipodean cousins. The
influence of free-market values and logics of competition have
been conditioned in the United Kingdom by the priorities of
their political advocates, not to mention the extant political
culture of 'declinism' and the continuing purchase of moral
economies of education inimical to logics of competition
(which might be characterised in part as the 'comprehensive
legacy') (Finn M., 2018a, 2018b).

But this is not to say that free market values and the logic
of competition have not been present in Britain's political culture over the past several decades. Quite the contrary. They
have shaped its discursive vocabulary and constructed the
very nature of higher education reform. In fact, part of
the need for the historicisation of the British university experience is to highlight how, in the United Kingdom, declinism
and technocracy (Edgerton, 2005) acted as *catalysts* for neoliberal reform. Declinism and technocracy predated the 'crisis
of Keynesianism' and the adoption of neoliberal policies
by the Callaghan and Thatcher governments (Davies W.,
2017). And there are other factors — such as the cultural
purchase of class in Britain and its subtle politicisation of
everyday life — which also have to be accounted for
(Lawrence, 2000). Yet it is the contention of this chapter that
universities in the United Kingdom have a peculiar reflexive
relationship to neoliberal political economy which helps to
explain many of their travails in the Brexit moment. For
Davies, Brexit is a revolt against the prevailing norms of

neoliberalism, most specifically the logic of competition which divides the population into 'winners' and 'losers'.

> ... at the bare minimum, organising social relations in terms of 'competition' means that individuals, organisations, cities, regions and nations are to be tested in terms of their capacity to out-do each other. Not only that, but the tests must be considered fair in some way, if the resulting inequalities are to be recognised as legitimate. When applied to individuals, this ideology is often known as 'meritocracy'. (Davies W., 2017, p. xvi)

The rules of the game ensure that 'success and prowess are things that are earned through desire, effort and innate ability ...':

> But the corollary of this is that failure and weakness are also earned: when individuals and communities fail to succeed, this is a reflection of inadequate talent or energy on their part. (Davies W., 2017, p. xvi)

The result, as in Michael Young's original *Rise of the Meritocracy* (Young, 1958), is 'revolt' — the revolt in this case being manifested the Brexit vote, which epitomised the 'revenge of politics on economics' (Davies W., 2017, p. xiv). The Brexit moment, when expert advice was rejected and a gulf of understanding recognised between universities and the broader public, was the moment when:

> ... a moral-economic system aimed at identifying and empowering the most competitive people, institutions and places has become targeted, rationally or otherwise, by the vast number of people, institutions

and places that have suffered not only the pain of
defeat but the punishment of defeat for far too long.
(Davies W., 2017, p. xviii)

The 'education gap' Runciman identified in relation to the
politics of the Brexit moment has profound implications for
universities, who find themselves on the wrong side of what
can be (crudely) constructed as a democratic/technocratic
divide. This was well illustrated by the fate of academic
expertise during the referendum debate.

OUT OF TOUCH? EXPERTS, ELITES AND MASS HIGHER EDUCATION

Academics have always occupied a privileged position in
British public life; many of the 'public moralists' featured in
Stefan Collini's eponymous account of Victorian England
were based in universities (Collini, 1991), whilst in the post-
war period academic intellectuals and scientists were influential in shaping the output of the British Broadcasting
Corporation (BBC) (Jones, 2014). In the post-war age of the
'technocratic moment' (Edgerton, 2005, p. 191), there was a
nexus of academic—political crossover. During the war years,
many academics (including the doyen of British higher
education, Lionel Robbins) found themselves drafted into
government service (Hennessy, 1989). A number of post-war
politicians, including Cabinet ministers such as Harold
Wilson, Tony Crosland, Richard Crossman, Keith Joseph
and Enoch Powell, had been academics themselves. Whilst
the stereotype of the 'remote and ineffectual don' persisted in
English culture in particular (at least in part the legacy of
fictional depictions such as Kingsley Amis' *Lucky Jim*), academics were influential in both political and popular culture.

With the advent of television, academics became a constant feature of documentary serials, leading to the contemporary phenomenon of John Smyth's 'academic rock star' (Smyth, 2017), the TV academic who enters the domain of celebrity through their work, a group that includes figures such as the anatomist Professor Alice Roberts, the classicist Professor Mary Beard and the physicist Professor Brian Cox.

Academic influence on political culture has been profound, and almost impossible to delimit definitively. The publication of studies into a range of social, cultural and political issues has become staple fare of the news cycle, in the United Kingdom as in the rest of the world, and this has had a reflexive impact on research itself. Research that seeks to attain 'impact' — now a criterion of assessment in contemporary research audit — is often designed to do so in the first place. The Research Councils now award significant grant funding via 'Impact Acceleration Accounts' which are tailored towards:

> … strengthening user engagement … strengthening the exchange of knowledge through culture and capability development, including through the development of skills for KE [knowledge exchange] activity; supporting knowledge exchange and commercialisation at early stages of progressing research outputs and outcomes to the point when they would be supported by other funding; supporting new, innovative and imaginative approaches to KE and Impact, including processes that enable 'fast failure' and appropriate learning; supporting activities that enable impact to be achieved in an effective and timely manner, including secondments and people exchange. (Research Councils UK, 2014)

In the initial decisions on the forthcoming REF2021 audit exercise, the proportion of weighting afforded to 'impact' has increased, whilst that afforded to the quality of the research itself has decreased (HEFCE, 2017). But the Brexit moment delivered an existential shock to the experts in the academic community, which overwhelmingly supported the cause of remaining in the European Union. As the President of the Royal Historical Society Peter Mandler noted, the more such academics attempted to influence public debate from a position of expertise, the more they reinforced a perception of themselves as on the wrong side of a popular/elite divide (Mandler, 2016). Michael Gove's infamous cry during the referendum campaign that Britain had 'had enough of experts' appeared to emblematise a public sphere which now rejected appeals to authority rooted in such expertise (Mance, 2016). In Trumpian vein, Gove delegitimised the legions of opposing expertise by claiming that such experts had 'done very well' out of the EU, and represented a vested interest. This echoed LSE academic and UKIP founder Alan Sked's comments to the same effect which the LSE Commission on the Future of Britain in Europe described as 'snide' (Corbett, 2016, p. 17). Yet Sked's comments were evocative of the tenor of the debate which was to follow.

When the University of Liverpool law Professor Michael Dougan produced an online lecture on the referendum, it received over seven million views on Facebook — clearly demonstrating a continued engagement with expertise on the part of the public (Connelly, 2016). However, Dougan also received a considerable number of abusive e-mails and death threats, with direct accusations that he had been 'bought' by the European Union. He was told by one correspondent that they hoped that Dougan would see his children die of cancer.

Dr Mike Galsworthy, co-founder of Scientists for EU, told *The Independent* newspaper that

> There's this big culture of distrust towards the authorities and people who know their areas …. We are used to being trusted … on our Facebook page, there was a lot of cynicism about 'vested interests, you're all bought out by the EU, shame on you for thinking of yourself before British democracy'. (Johnston, 2016)

Dougan argued that the Leave campaign ('the most dishonest political campaign in modern British history') mounted an assault on the 'most important values which the academic profession is entrusted to represent and defend'. His critique is worth quoting at length:

> [T]he commitment to pragmatic, rational, evidence-based scientific investigation, which seeks to inform and better our society through the cultivation of expert skill, knowledge and experience, to be tested and refined through a process of objective and rigorous peer review. It is simply impossible to reconcile those values with a politics which is proudly ideological and, with it, indifferent to evidence, immune to persuasion, cynically selective and self-serving in its analysis, and ultimately anti-democratic in its intolerance of dissent.
>
> That irreconcilable conflict perhaps helps to explain the ferocity of the attack which so many Leave campaigners (in particular) launched against so many academics … who volunteered to perform the public service of participating in various debates surrounding the 2016 referendum. (Dougan, 2017a, p. 6)

Dougan further highlights that one of the problems posed by the 'impact agenda' driven by research assessment is the vulnerability of academics who it exposes — whose e-mail addresses, office locations and even office hours are freely available online — to 'politically motivated hostility' (Dougan, 2017a, p. 7). In his own experience, he noted that

> There was also the experience of meeting lots of people who were not interested in the slightest in anything I had to say as soon as they realised it wasn't going to confirm their pre-existing viewpoints ... That professionally can be quite a strange sensation, because we're used to working in an environment with people who are open-minded, who like to be challenged, who like to hear different points of view, and when you come across relatively-large numbers of people who simply refuse to listen to a word that you say, often on the basis of highly spurious reasons for confirming their own unwillingness to listen to you, that's quite a professional challenge I think. (Dougan, 2017b)

Writing on Brexit and Trump has begun to address the plight of expertise, alongside the proliferation of 'fake news' and 'alternative facts' in a supposed-era of 'post-truth' politics (d'Ancona, 2017; Davis, 2017; Sayer, 2017; Suiter, 2016; Thompson, 2016). The account presented here focuses only on one aspect in a specific context — that of the situation of academic experts in British universities. Much has been said and more will be elsewhere on the role of social media in changing the nature of the public sphere, the crisis of trust in prevailing political/social authority, the willingness of politicians to drink from the well of populism and anti-establishment sentiment (or, as Thompson views it, the return of demagoguery). These factors may well be of far greater significance to the overall political culture of the Brexit moment than the role of academic expertise and the situation of universities (Finn M., 2019). But the nature of the Brexit moment is illustrative of the relationship between universities and broader society. Whilst academics were shocked by the level of hostility their pronouncements met with, the Brexit moment did not represent a disjuncture in terms of their relationship with society but a profound illustration of its true nature. It reflected the changed place of the university into an engine of Cannadine's 'dichotomous' class relations (Cannadine, 1998), the 'us' and 'them' of graduate and non-graduate, educated and (supposedly) uneducated. As much as anything else, the expansion of higher education to an authentically 'mass' system in the years after 1992 saw the transition of the university degree to a 'positional good' both in terms of *economic* capital, but more profoundly, in terms of *cultural* capital too. In contemporary Britain, a university degree is increasingly the *sina qua non* of middle-class respectability. This transition has taken place over several decades, and hit the elite first. In the course of the James Bond film franchise which began with *Dr. No* in 1962, 007 went from Eton dropout to (in the afterglow of Robbins) a Cambridge graduate in Oriental Languages. As the 1960s drew to a close, it was no longer plausible that Britain's superspy — the epitome of a reified vision of the upper middle-class — could be without a university education.

But even in 2017, the majority of the UK population do not attend university. In part, the challenge posed to the place of expertise in the public sphere represented the success of the UK higher education expansion programme — and its failure. By 2015, the Higher Education Initial Participation Rate for English people — that proportion of those below the age of

30 having experienced higher education — hits 48% (Department for Education, 2016). Almost half the English population under the age of 30 were thought to have attended university. But that meant more than half of them still hadn't. When higher education had been an elite concern, it did not represent a 'dichotomous' class divide. Though class exclusion and inequalities of cultural capital were not merely real, but very much more so at that time, mass higher education as it has developed in England in particular has resulted the near-even split of the English population into an 'us and them' who encounter each other on a regular basis. With education, and particularly higher education, conferring cultural capital above and beyond its supposed economic benefits, this inevitably fostered a sense of injustice and inequality which was tangible. As the present author has written elsewhere:

> Universities became an industry at least in part because for many middle-class families higher education was by now a standard marker of cultural capital; in an era of mass higher education, 'not going to uni' was the ultimate cultural marker in Britain's (still) class-ridden society, succeeding the failure of the 11+ as the great stigma of the post-war era. (Finn M., 2015c, p. 97)

Generationally speaking, those above the age of 30 were increasingly likely — as age category moved on — not to have attended higher education. This correlated with an increasing likelihood to have voted to Leave the European Union. When a team of Warwick economists analysed the motivations of referendum voters, they noted a strong correlation between levels of education and Remain/Leave support (Becker, Fetzer, & Novy, 2016). Whilst they concluded that lower levels of formal education correlated with Leave voting, they noticed another interesting feature in their dataset; that in the areas where the numbers with higher qualifications had grown most sharply (often from a low base) there had been a stronger Leave vote (Becker et al., 2016, p. 23). This may, as the authors note, simply illustrate greater population growth in those areas and attendant pressure on services. However, in light of the wider discussion on the 'education gap' here, it might highlight the impact of sharper social division by education and life-chances on voter mobilisation and popular resentment. More detailed work will be required to find out which.

In general, Leave voters did not trust academics, whilst Remain voters did. Nearly 70% of Remain voters claimed to trust academics; only 26% of Leave voters did (YouGov, 2016). Higher education is, of course, only part of a package in terms of 'life chances', but it is a significant part. Sixty per cent of London residents are now graduates — a rate much higher than elsewhere in the United Kingdom, such as the Leave-voting North East, only 29% of whom were graduates (Office for National Statistics, 2013). And though higher education was a significant indicator of voter persuasion in the 2016 referendum, it was a variable that was internally diffuse. Life chances varied again depending on university and course attended. Just as there was a class hierarchy between university graduates and those who entered the world of work directly on leaving school, there was also a class hierarchy within the higher education system itself. Some academics commented that this applied to the academic profession, no less than to students. Lisa Mckenzie, an ethnographer and research fellow in the sociology department at the LSE commented:

> Over the past year and a bit, I have watched the academic world (in all disciplines) flail around at Brexit,

at Donald Trump and, this summer, at the Grenfell
Tower fire. 'How could these tragedies have hap-
pened?' they cry ... But the truth is clear for any of
us who have come from working-class families and
communities: the middle-class academic elite are
totally out of touch. And no balancing of their surveys is going to change that. It is clear that this middle-class, liberal, highly educated section of society
did not see these events coming. (Mckenzie, 2017b)

Academic expertise was thus on the wrong side of a class
divide, but it had also been subject to politically motivated
attacks of increasing vigour even prior to the referendum
debate. Vote Leave leader Michael Gove had spent some
years both before and during his tenure as Education
Secretary launching a series of attacks on expertise and academia, drawing on classic neoliberal tropes of 'vested interest'. In the realm of teacher education, he had overseen a
series of sustained attacks on university-based initial teacher
education, characterising the academic educational research
community as part of the 'blob' holding back school performance (Finn M., 2015a, 2015b, p. 5). In this discursive framing, he synthesised traditional neoliberal views on producer
interest with an assault on the social sciences more generally.
Though Gove encouraged 'research', he reconceptualised it as
being led by teachers and outside the university environment.
Gove himself conceived of such research in terms of a 'real-
world'/ivory tower dichotomy that was also championed
by authors such as Robert Peal (2014) and a number of
figures associated with the think-tanks Policy Exchange and
Civitas. As Gove put it in a speech to Policy Exchange in 2013:

In the past, the education debate has been dominated by education academics - which is why so

> much of the research and evidence on how children
> actually learn has been so poor ... Now, thankfully,
> teachers are taking control of their profession's intel-
> lectual life, taking the lead in pioneering educational
> research and creating a living evidence base. (Gove,
> 2013)

The key element was to marginalise university-based expertise in favour narratives framed in terms of lived experience, in the vein of Tony Blair's non-ideology ideology; 'what works' (Labour Party, 1997). Gove's behaviour in this regard helped shape the discursive politics of the Brexit moment. Gove had always conceived of himself as an historian, and championed a particular conception of Britishness anchored in a Protestant identity hostile to Catholic Europe (Gove, Mrs May is our first Catholic Prime Minister, 2017). He endorsed a campaign by Civitas to restore narrative history teaching to British schools, and in particular the history of Britain and its Empire. For Civitas, this included sponsoring the republica-tion and dissemination of Henrietta Barnett's imperialist mythology *Our Island Story (Wellings, 2016)*. Gove's celebra-tory approach to British imperial history chimed with the UK population's views as a whole; in 2014, less than a fortnight after Gove was sacked as Education Secretary, a YouGov sur-vey revealed that 59% of the British population felt the Empire was 'something to be proud of' (Dahlgreen, 2016). As leaders in the Vote Leave campaign, both Gove and Boris Johnson made great use of populist historical mythologies — including the memory of the Second World War — to mobi-lise a Brexit constituency. Notwithstanding the best efforts of Historians for Britain IN Europe, such visions resonated far more widely than the views of professional historians.

The assault on expertise predated the Brexit moment, but in the referendum debate it found its most violent expression.

The response — particularly virulent online — to academics offering the benefit of their expertise begged a number of questions about the place of the university in public life. In an era where 'impact' conditions much of the funding and direction of research, what does this kind of interaction with a febrile public sphere tell us about the social function of the academy? In the referendum's wake a number of British universities — including Leeds and Warwick (Morland, 2017) — began attempts to remove employment protections from academic staff, allowing for dismissal on grounds such as 'some other substantial reason' (BBC News, 2017a, 2017b) or 'damaging the university's reputation' (Morland, 2017). The ability — and desire — of universities and their staff to speak truth to power is an increasingly open question in the Brexit moment.

THE CONSUMER AND THE 'CULTURE OF SUSPICION'

Universities had become increasingly marketized in the period after 1998, which left them vulnerable to what Onora O'Neill calls 'a culture of suspicion' (O'Neill, 2002). Part of the success of the government's policy of 'steering' higher education through market mechanisms lays in the transfer of the practice of active suspicion from the agencies of the state (though those agencies nonetheless played their part) to a mass constituency of student-consumers, much more able to apply pressure to institutions directly. Though these trends were continuous in the period after 1998, the transfer of the funding burden for higher education from the taxpayer to the student in the Browne Review, coupled with the near-annihilation of state subsidy for undergraduate teaching in many subjects, ensured an acceleration of the development of audit processes (some of which O'Neill herself had lamented in her 2002 Reith Lectures) (O'Neill, 2002).

The arrival of the National Student Survey (NSS) in 2005 was followed in the Browne era by the TEF from 2017, which included NSS data in determining its conclusions as to whether universities — more properly referred to as 'providers' (as under the new legislative framework they were not required to be universities *per se*) — could allocate 'medals' of Gold, Silver and Bronze at the institutional level (*Times Higher Education*, 2017). That the idea of awarding such accolades at institutional level, presupposing a universal standard of teaching, was straightforwardly and inevitably inaccurate, was widely recognised. The other significant criticism — that the TEF's auditing mechanisms relied on proxies rather than any direct evaluation of the quality of teaching — was acknowledged by the chair of the TEF (Husbands, 2017). Nonetheless the TEF pressed on. But as O'Neill had observed 15 years earlier, the introduction of such accountability measures across the public realm has not served to restore trust, but rather to increase suspicion — not least due to the inevitable introduction of perverse incentives which promotes 'gaming'; engaging in activities that will serve to 'do well in the TEF' rather than serving the university's mission of education and scholarship (Franco-Santos & Otley, 2017). The summer of 2017, the summer when the first TEF results were published, saw arguably some of the most sustained 'bad press' for universities since the 1980s, and was described by one higher education journalist as a 'public relations disaster' (Morris D., 2017c). Rather than reassuring the public sphere as to the quality of university teaching, the very existence of the TEF appeared to reinforce the view that universities were, by their very nature, 'suspect' institutions, views echoed in the *Timebomb* report produced by UK2020.

Tice, al-Humaidi, Seldon and Adonis' broadsides are classic neoliberal discourse, and they rest on the assumption — made quite frankly in Seldon's interventions — that students not only are consumers, but they should be. This is where universities are culpable in their own construction. Too often, university leaderships have been willing to accept the student–consumer dynamic in order to succeed in the competitive world of rankings and recognition. Too many individual academics have forgotten that neoliberal discourse is not an anterior force oppressing an academic population all by itself, but an embodied reality constituted by academic acceptance and enunciation. The competitive individual academic (including the present author), seeking recognition through REF, NSS and others, has become the perfect neoliberal vehicle for the remaking of the institution in terms of values the academic claims not to respect. The historian Emilie Murphy, writing in the aftermath of the TEF results, condemned such academic 'hypocrisy':

> Considering how long academics, and students, have decried the metrics that underpin the assessment it was hugely frustrating to see universities widely celebrating their new shiny gold and silver medals on social media. What made this even worse was to witness colleagues from multiple institutions – especially those who have challenged TEF methodology in the past – widely sharing their university ratings with pride. Their hypocrisy was galling.
> (Murphy, 2017)

The late critic and cultural studies scholar Mark Fisher (who had trained at Warwick and was based at Goldsmith's) compared developments in school- and college-level education with university audit culture:

> The changes in OFSTED inspections are mirrored by
> in the change from the Research Assessment
> Exercise to the Research Excellence Framework in
> higher education: periodic assessment will be super-
> seded by a permanent and ubiquitous measurement
> which cannot help but generate the same perpetual
> anxiety. (Fisher M., 2009, pp. 51–52)

Fisher further remarked on the hypocrisies that were necessary in educational institutions to maintain this system in
operation, focusing on the example of his sometime line-
manager:

> the preservation of his 60s liberal self-image
> depended upon his 'not really believing' in the audit-
> ing processes he so assiduously enforced. What this
> disavowal depends upon is the distinction between
> inner subjective attitude and outward
> behaviour … in terms of his inner subjective atti-
> tude, the manager is hostile, even contemptuous,
> towards, the bureaucratic procedures he supervises;
> but in terms of his outward behavior, he is perfectly
> compliant. (Fisher M., 2009, p. 55)

In embodying the practises of the discourses academics claim
to oppose, they have played their part in entrenching the new
culture of the university in public space. In other words, by
failing to articulate an alternative notion of the university in
practice as much as at the level of critique, the academic
community has, to a great extent, abdicated the field in
publicly defining what universities are for. With universities
conceived of in terms of the student consumer, additional
non-state-sponsored indices of the student experience now
proliferate, fostering expectations of the 'student experience'
that universities simply cannot deliver on their extant model.

A HEPI survey in 2017 highlighted that prospective under-graduates now expect a greater number of contact hours than they had received in school, highlighting the failure of univer-sities to sufficiently articulate what it is which differentiates them to schools, either to their prospective students, or to policymakers (HEPI, 2017).

The commodification of higher education in the public sphere, coupled with its strong associations with class and cultural capital, effectively disenfranchised much of its exper-tise in the Brexit moment. In terms of this last, the work of the ethnographer Lisa Mckenzie implies, for many amongst Leave-voting communities, the university could not be further away:

> The people who participated in my study, like others
> in similarly excluded positions ... could only 'trade'
> in social and cultural capital that had very little
> worth beyond the bounds of their own local
> communities ... the sum-total of the leave-voting
> 'locals' was enough to outnumber the 'cosmopolitan'
> 'Remainers'; typically these Remainers are middle
> class, urban, white-collar professionals and who
> possess economic, social and cultural capital of
> much broader value .... (Mckenzie, 2017a, p. 202)

This had particular consequences at individual, disciplinary levels — historians were unable to make effective interven-tions, and political scientists profoundly misread the mood of the nation. Expertise had, instead, become suspect — and was valuable, like the rest of higher education, primarily as a consumption good in a buyer's market.

The crises of the Brexit moment for British higher educa-tion had their roots overall in a profound crisis of trust in the authority of the university and its academic citizens. In some small part, despite many noble efforts on the part of individuals, that was a measure of dereliction of duty from those citizens in terms of fighting hard enough in their daily practice for the vision of the university they professed to espouse. The consequences of this crisis of trust are still being played out, but this crisis is fundamental to the new political economy of higher education in contemporary Britain.

PART III

CONCLUSIONS

CHAPTER FIVE

CONCLUSION: THE POLITICAL ECONOMY OF HIGHER EDUCATION IN BREXIT BRITAIN

*... we need to confront the possibility of some insti-
tutions choosing — or needing — to exit the market.
This is a crucial part of a healthy, competitive and
well-functioning market, and such exits happen
already — although not frequently — in the higher
education sector. The Government should not prevent exit as a matter of policy.*

Department for Business, Innovation and Skills,
*Success as a Knowledge Economy: Teaching excellence,
social mobility and student choice* (2016b, p. 38).

*The accepted view of the way a higher education
system functions is that it is national.*

— LSE Commission on the Future of Britain and Europe,
*Higher Education and Research: Report of the hearing
held on December 8, 2015* (2016), p. 6

*In the Brexit vote outcome, higher education and
research have become collateral damage of the larger*

> *issues contained in national identity and Brexit. No-one*
> *really targeted higher education or wanted it to be*
> *damaged, aside from the second-order hostility towards*
> *academic experts as part of the established elite. For*
> *most people voting in the referendum, they simply were*
> *not thinking about the effects on higher education and*
> *research. But damage will occur, nonetheless.*

Professor Simon Marginson, *Times Higher Education*,
13 September 2017 (2017a)

A POLITICAL, ECONOMIC AND CULTURAL IMPLICATION: THE IDEA OF A UNIVERSITY IN THE BREXIT MOMENT

The language of the British state, David Edgerton reminds us, is the language of political economy (Edgerton, 2005). So too the policy *lingua franca* of its university system. Though Brexit threatened huge discontinuity for an avowedly-internationalist higher education system and research community, in that one respect the Brexit moment maintained clear continuity with the past. The language of contemporary higher education policy remained that of political economy, and policy reform in this vein proceeded largely undisturbed. Despite calls for a pause, the Higher Education and Research Bill became an Act of Parliament and thence law in the United Kingdom a year on from the referendum. The long-awaited TEF produced its results exactly one day short of the referendum's first anniversary. As we have seen, in the words of one vice-chancellor on government higher education policy in the Brexit moment, things really had just 'carried on regardless' (Croft, 2017).

This continuity will make things easier for future historians of British higher education, who will wish to trace the development of marketisation within the British system, amongst other things. But it will also beg other questions, and may in time become an interesting case study. The obvious counterfactual question will be why? Why did government choose *not* to pause its ambitions for higher education reforms in the Brexit moment, but instead elect to proceed with a wholesale restructure of the higher education landscape — the most profound in a quarter of a century — against a background of huge economic and political uncertainty? As this short book has shown, the answer lies in the nature of the evolution of Britain's higher education system and its own reflexive relationship with the Brexit moment. In terms of a case study, higher education policy in Britain is illustrative both of the specificity of Britain's engagement with the economic and political imaginary oft-referenced as 'neoliberalism', and of this particular imaginary's resilience in the face of Harold Macmillan's much-vaunted 'events'. Notwithstanding John Smyth's claim that neoliberalism is now a 'zombie' ideology (Smyth, 2017), market values and the logic of competition remains at the heart of British higher education, even in the light of the exogenous shock of Brexit.

In terms of the specificity of Britain's engagement with neoliberalism, this in turn helps illustrate both the development of Britain's universities and the nature of the Brexit moment. Brexit itself has been regarded by some writing from the point of view of contemporary history (including this author) as a creature of Britain's post-war 'declinist' political culture (Finn M., 2019). This was a Britain which in the decades following the Second World War transformed its higher education system in order to maximise its human capital in a more-or-less desperate attempt to retain global political power. The decision to join the European Union's predecessor was taken on a 'transactional' basis (Marginson, 2017a); it was an attempt to retain as much world influence as possible for the United Kingdom in light of Britain's inability to foster an alternative economic unit. When Britain ultimately elected to leave the European Union in June 2016, this was for some at least of its protagonists part of the same process; the revival of the 'Anglosphere' (Bell, 2017) and the evocation of imperial nostalgia (Finn M., 2016b) which characterised the referendum debate espoused different answers to the same problem — the problem of decline. For some of Britain's policymakers, the empire wasn't over, at least not yet.

The language of government since the referendum outcome — if not before — has been the language of nationalism, in keeping with the declinist paradigm. Insofar as government has set out its ambitions for higher education in explicit connection with the Brexit process, these ambitions have been nationalistic. In this, there is a continuity, both with prior policy and the general political economy of British higher education as envisaged by policymakers. Though academics and students may have seen their institutions and ambitions as international, successive governments — from the Attlee Government of 1945 onward — have seen universities as national assets in a zero-sum game of global competition. Britain was hardly unique in this, but the linkage between higher education and national interest was stronger and more profound in Britain given the purchase of 'declinism'; the cultural trope that mourned the loss of Empire which — translated into political action — sought to maintain a world role.

Yet during the post-war period, as we saw in Chapter One, there was a consistent contest between idealist conceptions of higher education that espoused education for a free society and an 'active' citizenry, and economistic understandings of the value of higher education which couched the ambitions of policy in terms of benefit to the

economy and by extension, British power. Left at that however, such an account is an oversimplification. What took
place in higher education policy was a dialogue between
moral economies of higher education and political economies;
both categories evolved over time, but in the realm of the
former lay the clarion call of 'free higher education'.

'Free higher education', and education for a free society,
were noble visions put forward for the British university in
the post-war 'idealist moment'. The demise of 'education for
a free society' (if not the moral economy of free higher education, as Joseph Ibrahim, 2014 rightly notes) is an illustration
of one of the major cultural and political implications of the
Brexit moment — if not Brexit itself. This is the loss of
the universities' ability to define their own missions. Lionel
Robbins' interventions in the mid-1960s were the culmina-
tion of a two decades-long ferment, and they were couched in
terms of a broader benefit to society. Whilst Robbins con-
ceded the point (via a reference to Confucius) that few would
attend university without thought for their future employment, he did not concede that that was in fact the point of
higher education:

> … while emphasising that there is no betrayal of
> values when institutions of higher education teach
> what will be of some practical use, we must postu-
> late that what is taught should be taught in such a
> way as to promote the general powers of the mind.
> The aim should be to produce not mere specialists
> but rather cultivated men and women …
> (Committee on Higher Education, 1963, p. 7)

The 'advancement of learning' was also critical for Robbins:

> … the search for truth is an essential function of
> institutions of higher education and the process of

> education is itself most vital when it partakes of the
> nature of discovery. (Committee on Higher
> Education, 1963, p. 7)

The final purpose of higher education was, as Robbins noted,
'difficult to describe concisely':

> ... but that is none the less fundamental: the trans-
> mission of a common culture and common stan-
> dards of citizenship. By this we do not mean the
> forcing of all individuality into a common mould:
> that would be the negation of higher education as
> we conceive it. But we believe that it is a proper
> function of higher education, as of education in
> schools, to provide in partnership with the family
> that background of culture and social habit upon
> which a healthy society depends. This function,
> important at all times, is perhaps especially impor-
> tant in an age that has set for itself the ideal of
> equality of opportunity. It is not merely by providing
> places for students from all classes that this ideal
> will be achieved, but also by providing, in the
> atmosphere of the institutions in which the students
> live and work, influences that in some measure com-
> pensate for any inequalities of home background.
> These influences are not limited to the student
> population. Universities and colleges have an impor-
> tant role to play in the general cultural life of the
> communities in which they are situated. (Committee
> on Higher Education, 1963)

Robbins' belief that universities had such broad social functions to play in the national life was one reason why he was
so vehemently opposed to the Wilson Government's establishment of the polytechnic system (Robbins L., 1966a,

1966b). And he was not alone. Much of the British academic community's 'usable past', conceiving of higher education as a social and public good, stems from the arguments used by academic advocates of expansion in the immediate post-war period — arguments which were always contested, but never fully repudiated

In the realm of political economy lay the interventions by government in the sector to promote (in particular) science and technology, and the decisions made to marketise the sector from the later 1990s onward. The marketisation of higher education took root in quite the way it did in the United Kingdom for a variety of reasons, not least political expediency, but also because higher education was institutionally amenable to a 'remaking' through a political economy which espoused the benefits of globalisation. Universities, no less than UK financial services, embraced the internationalisation aspect of the neoliberal policy consensus, with the result that they became a 'world leading' sector by all of the indices used to 'rank' success in this sphere. As Simon Marginson puts it:

> The UK's two most successful global sectors are financial services, and higher education and research. Different though they are, each is likely to be collateral damage of blood and soil nationalist politics. (Marginson, 2017b)

But the 'massification' (Marginson, 2017b) of higher education in the United Kingdom had profound social, cultural and economic implications for British society as we have seen. As Marginson has put in relation to the United States and the United Kingdom:

> Degree holders concentrate in cities. In the UK, just 26 per cent of degree holders voted Leave, compared with 78 per cent of people without qualifications.

> Young people, the most educated generation in UK
> history, overwhelmingly voted Remain.
>
> In the US, Trump celebrated the 'uneducated' and
> secured a sharp swing among those who had never
> attended college. Clinton secured more than half the
> vote from only one group of white voters: college-
> educated women.
>
> It is ironic, isn't it? Once higher participation higher
> education, and also climate science, become more
> central, they can be used to polarise an electorate on
> the basis of identity. You can't divide an electorate
> this way when only 5 per cent of people go to uni-
> versity. (Marginson, 2017b)

Universities had always been implicated in the politics of
Britain's class system, but it has never been more true than in
the age of mass higher education. Though the political economy of higher education espoused the virtue of 'having a
degree' in terms of access to wage premium, the cultural capital which graduate status implied — even though it is internally highly diffuse — created a new fracture in British
society, the 'us' and 'them' of the graduate and non-graduate
populations.

Universities, their academic citizens, and their student
ones, thus became part of the 'them', even though they were
integral to a political economy of higher education that
sought to draw on them as a font of economic growth. In
this, they became part of the Brexit moment more broadly,
and constitutive of it. As we saw in Chapter Four, at least in
part Brexit was a revolt against the 'winners' of the neoliberal
political game, 'the revenge of politics', in William Davies'
expressive phrase (Davies W., 2017). And yet many students
did not see themselves as winners. Burdened with debt far

higher than previous generations of students endured, they were not, in truth, in receipt of the same 'deal' as those (relatively few) who had attended university in the three decades after Robbins. As they became consumers they — and their parents — became more focused on 'employability' and the instrumental aspect of the degree process, ever-conscious of a possible diminution of the wage premium due to the growing numbers of graduates. The consumer relationship became the driving, steering dynamic in higher education, and academic and student mental health alike went into crisis (*The Guardian*, 2017).

The government sought to press on with its reforms to higher education because, from the internal logic of these reforms, there was no reason not to. Undergraduate education was now conceived of in government policy documents as a form of higher secondary vocational education, whilst research was gradually sundered from it and repurposed in favour of STEM research aiming at commercialisation and patents for the good of the economy. Both of these were economic perspectives, which nominally represented the final triumph of the political economy of higher education as the organising framework for understanding the place of the university in Britain. The Brexit moment catalysed government action in the repurposing of higher education and added a more significant nationalist inflection in its political economy; in the government's industrial and innovation strategy the universities were seen as a patent-generating economic resource to be maximised in the post-Brexit world.

Yet even within its own terms, the political economy of higher education in Brexit Britain was riddled with contradictions. Whilst, as the LSE report noted, the conventional wisdom regarded university 'systems' in national terms, the truth, as we have seen, is that they are — if successful — international ones. The government's attitude to international partnership in the Brexit moment is inimical to their success, and inimical to their potential for supporting the UK economy in this time of crisis. And even prior to Brexit, government policy had had implications for the viability of subjects necessary for Britain's economic prosperity, notably modern languages. Given consistent arguments about the centrality of the wage premium and the nature of higher education as an investment, it was believed that this would change the degree subject profile within universities in favour of subjects beneficial to the wider economy — usually STEM. There is evidence that this was the case. The humanities had 42,000 fewer students in 2016 than in 2007; biological sciences had gained nearly 58,000 over the same period (Universities UK, 2017, p. 25). Modern languages had taken a major hit, with a decline of over 28,000 students, in age of globalisation and in a country not known for its proficiency in such languages (Universities UK, 2017, p. 25). This was damage which could only be exacerbated by wrong moves in the Brexit negotiations, with potential expulsion from ERASMUS calling into question many modern languages degree placement opportunities.

In the course of this account, we have seen that if a particular political-economic model holds sway in government, privileging market fundamentalism in policy development to the point of reconstructing much of the social and political world in terms of 'capitalist realism' (Fisher M., 2009), then events such as Brexit do not derail or unsettle policy trajectories (especially not when they themselves are reflexively linked to these trajectories). They do not 'limit' neoliberalism as a political imaginary, however much they may limit some of its policy ambitions in reality (Davies W., 2017). Despite the colossal blow Brexit dealt to the theory and practice of market integration, government was unwilling — or unable — to conceive of an alternate path for higher education to the one it had already set in train. As we saw in Chapter Four, in the aftermath of the Brexit vote, universities have come under significant pressure, both from figures within and without government. The inflated political diction characteristic of the Brexit moment has been turned on them, with former junior education minister Andrew Adonis turning his ire on them via the medium of Twitter. Adonis, citing the aforementioned *Sunday Times* story, claimed that universities were complicit in a 'betrayal' of British students by recruiting international ones (Knapton, 2017). Coupled with his personal *bêtes noires* of vice-chancellor pay and the absence of sufficient numbers (in his view) of two-year degrees, this was a form of treachery.

In light of this, it is easy to see why the Cambridge classicist Robin Osborne argues that the biggest concerns for British higher education in the near future stem from domestic sources:

> The broader landscape, the UKRI side, the pressures from government and so on — all of that looks much more depressing. And that's where … the undermining of respect for academic expertise, the revelations that there is really a very substantial body of people who simply, clearly, don't see the point of what we do, and the revelation that there is that body of voters who can be mobilised is clearly going to affect how political parties tailor their appeal. All of that is bad news. (Osborne, 2017)

As this book has shown then, the Brexit moment represents a broader malaise regarding universities' place in Britain's national life. Government and sections of society alike share instrumentalist views of universities; that they are essentially factories for the production of human capital. In August

2017, another Cambridge classicist, Professor Mary Beard, was criticised on Twitter after she attempted to publicly defend education for education's sake; a respondent — the founder of an educational social mobility organisation — argued that such a view of education was elitist, and represented 'privileged middle-class thinking' (Snell, 2017). It is not merely that education for education's sake is navel-gazing, according to some critics — it is also morally wrong.

So, in sum, what are the other implications for Britain's universities in this 'moment' in British political culture? Some are more or less obvious. Those addressed in Part I, the possible 'impacts' of a real rupture with Europe in terms of British universities' makeup or their research and the funding which supports it, have profound implications across the three spheres under discussion. At an economic level, the loss of extant flows of students and researchers to the United Kingdom from the EU will impoverish British institutions financially. But this example points up the fact that such issues do not remain in one sphere only; it will also impoverish British universities in intellectual and cultural terms, too. But on the economic level, such a sundering will not only impoverish British institutions, but the hinterlands they support. Whilst the cultural values of British universities may have been rejected by much of the public as part of the Brexit revolt, it remains the case that they were hitherto outposts of economic stability in many areas (particularly in the north of England, the Midlands, Wales and Northern Ireland) where other industries had collapsed. Damage to these institutions will damage the wider British economy, and it may do so differentially by region.

Culturally, universities find themselves adrift across a gulf from a large section of the public. At the level of Britain's relationship with Europe, and the universities' own relationships — the fundamental question of the referendum vote at the macro-level, and its sectoral impact below — universities failed to articulate an effective case for remaining in the union because they no longer knew how to effectively influence public discourse at the level of *values*. As higher education was reformed since the 1990s in the direction of a consumer model, universities — often so-called 'leading' universities — were keen to play up the 'consumer' benefits of their institutions. When Labour governments conceptualised the primary benefit of higher education as a 'wage premium', dissenting voices in the academy abounded, but too many university 'leaders' — whilst bemoaning such crude utilitarianism — nonetheless developed marketing strategies to show how their institution would deliver the best rate of return on the cash investment. Whilst academics privately condemn league tables, rankings and audit regimes such as the REF or the TEF, they nonetheless take to Twitter with enthusiasm to celebrate their 5* rating or their Gold award, while gossiping amongst themselves as to the failings of those who have failed to attain such distinction. As such, academics and their institutions have become prisoners of a discourse not of their own making, in a game they cannot win, redefining the mission for universities which many of them purport to believe in if not out of existence, then at least out of public view.

So, when the time came for universities to argue for Britain remaining in the EU, some groups — such as Scientists for EU — were quick to argue for collaboration as a key frame. Universities for Europe and university lobby groups all-too-often fell into the trap of talking mostly about funding; universities in general did not have their courage of their convictions to argue for a 'republic or science' or a frontierless 'republic of mind.' This allowed them to be constructed, and consequently delegitimised, as simply seeking to feather their own nests.

This failure — which highlights the marginalisation of universities at a cultural level in some parts of the United Kingdom — also has economic implications too. Any withdrawal from the Union which necessitates a concomitant withdrawal from Horizon 2020 and successor programmes will have serious financial implications. And it will also have huge further cultural and economic implications for collaboration and knowledge transfer. Any withdrawal from the Union which necessitates withdrawal from the ERASMUS+ scheme will have implications for collaboration too, not to mention specific — and serious — implications for placement arrangements for UK students undertaking Modern Languages courses as we saw above. But, more seriously even than this, it will damage the cosmopolitan nature of Britain's university campuses. It will remove a significant element of international cultural exchange which benefits British undergraduates who never leave their home institution for study. As the University Grants Committee put it in 1921:

> Provision for common life and intercourse is of the highest value in a university education. Not only is the intellectual training of students apt to be stunted if they remain as isolated units after leaving the classroom... (Murray, 1957, p. v)

Sir Keith Murray, chairman of the UGC in the 1950s, wrote in his Foreword to the 1957 Niblett Report on halls of residence that much of university education rested in the 'interplay of mind upon mind' (Murray, 1957, p. v). The subcommittee themselves believed this wider aspect of education should include social mixing and the 'encouragement to appreciate and discuss matters of the spirt and the intellect ... [including] religion, art, music, politics, current affairs and the relationship between human beings with an ultimate objective to "work out a philosophy of life" (University Grants Committee, 1957, p. 1). Such goals are seldom enunciated so clearly today, but there is no doubt that the introduction of a substantial number of European students via the ERASMUS scheme has helped fulfil them; this is the scale of the loss that students will suffer if it is withdrawn. It is intangible, perhaps, in that it cannot be counted in the same way as the 'wage premium' (although, as the EU has shown, the number of babies can be), but the benefits which accrue both to students and to wider society are then both literally and in a broader sense, incalculable.

CONCLUSION

This book has addressed the place of British universities in wider society in the Brexit moment, and the material impacts the UK's withdrawal from the European Union may have on them. At time of writing, they stand under constant attack for supposed-largesse, failure to deliver social mobility, remove from the priorities of the state and much else besides. They are undeniably in crisis. Some of this, as this book has argued, is of their own making; the academic profession in particular having failed to consistently articulate a clear vision for the university, and instead — in many cases, not least those of vice-chancellors — have 'played the game'. This has been a mistake. The most profound implication of the Brexit moment for Britain's universities is the crisis of trust they face. It is in terms of this aspect that the Brexit moment has highlighted the extent to which British universities have allowed themselves to be reconceived simply as service-providing businesses, rather than guardians of culture and criticism. In accepting this role, they have abdicated much of their post-war responsibility to intervene positively for the good of wider society. More than this, they have become an engine of stratification in a 'dichotomous' (Cannadine, 1998) class structure, cut off from half the population. Whilst they have been international in outlook, all-too-often many of them have failed to be 'civic'. This may be changing. Historians have begun playing closer attention to the civic traditions of Britain's universities (Whyte, 2015), providing a platform for their reassertion by the academics of today. Sociologists have begun to argue for a new 'guild' of academics (Lybeck, 2017), who will reclaim the university for an academic mission in the 'university of the future'. And academics of all stripes have promoted new, 'co-operative' models of higher education which seek to transcend the gulf between the marketised university and the public (Winn, 2014). But in the immediate future, the tasks remain twofold. Firstly, to rebuild trust between academic citizens, their institutions and the broader publics they serve. Finally, to preserve as much as possible of the European and international dimension of higher education in the vein of a genuine republic of science; otherwise the Brexit moment will not merely impoverish the culture of Britain's universities, but the culture and democracy of Britain as a whole.

REFERENCES

Adams, J. (2012, October 18). The rise of research networks. *Nature, 490.*

Adams, J. (2017). *International research collaboration after the UK leaves the European Union.* London: Universities UK.

Adonis, A. (2017). Is abolishing tuition fees regressive? It depends on how its done. *Times Higher Education*, August 17. Retrieved from https://www.timeshighereducation.com/opinion/abolishing-tuition-fees-regressive-it-depends-how-its-done

Allegretti, A. (2017). Open Britain exposes all the times Brexiters promised we wouldn't leave the single market. *Huffington Post*, January 19. Retrieved from http://www.huffingtonpost.co.uk/entry/open-britain-video-single-market-nigel-farage-anna-soubry_uk_582ce0a0e4b09025ba310fce

Allen, K., Treanor, J., & Goodley, S. (2016). Pound slumps to 31-year low following Brexit vote. *The Guardian*, June 24, 2016.

Arthur, M. (2016). British universities and Brexit (M. Finn, Interviewer), June 7.

Aschroft, M. (2016). *How the UK voted.* London: Lord Ashcroft Polls. Retrieved from http://lordashcroftpolls.com/wp-content/uploads/2016/06/How-the-UK-voted-Full-tables-1.pdf

Asthana, A., Stewart, H., & Vaughan, A. (2017). Ministers act to head off revolt over membership of European nuclear regulator. *The Guardian*, July 10. Retrieved from https://www.theguardian.com/politics/2017/jul/10/brexit-pm-making-plans-to-replicate-membership-of-atomic-energy-group-euratom

Baker, S. (2017a). Which subjects at UK universities rely most on EU academics? *Times Higher Education*, August 14. Retrieved from https://www.timeshighereducation.com/data-bites/which-subjects-uk-universities-rely-most-eu-academics

Baker, S. (2017b). Russell Group universities 'vulnerable' to Brexit brain drain. *Times Higher Education*, May 7. Retrieved from https://www.timeshighereducation.com/news/russell-group-universities-vulnerable-to-brexit-brain-drain

Ball, S. J. (1993). What is policy? Texts, trajectories and tool-boxes. *Discourse: Studies in the cultural politics of education*, *13*(2).

Ball, S. J. (2008). *The education debate*. Bristol: Policy Press.

Ball, S. J. (2017). *The education debate* (3rd ed.). Bristol: Policy Press.

Barlow Committee. (1946). *Scientific man-power: Report of a committee appointed by the Lord President of the Council*. London: HMSO.

Baurdrillard, J. (1994). *Simulacra and simulation*. Ann Arbor, MI: University of Michigan Press.

BBC News. (2004). *Graduates 'satisifed with jobs'. BBC News*. Retrieved from http://news.bbc.co.uk/1/hi/education/3808111.stm

BBC News. (2017a). Brexit: Theresa May's offer to EU citizens 'falls short'. *BBC News*, July 10. Retrieved from http://www.bbc.co.uk/news/uk-politics-40552318

BBC News. (2017b). Leeds University staff strike over dismissal policy changes. *BBC News*, June 22. Retrieved from http://www.bbc.co.uk/news/uk-england-leeds-40366011

Becker, S. O., Fetzer, T., & Novy, D. (2016). *Who voted for Brexit? A comprehensive district-level analysis*. Coventry: University of Warwick. Retrieved from http://www2.warwick.ac.uk/fac/soc/economics/research/centres/cage/manage/publications/305-2016_becker_fetzer_novy.pdf

Begley, C. (2016). *Written evidence to House of Commons Education Committee inquiry*, November.

Bell, D. (2017). The Anglosphere: New enthusiasm for an old dream. *Prospect*, Feburary. Retrieved from https://www.prospectmagazine.co.uk/magazine/anglosphere-old-dream-brexit-role-in-the-world

Bennett, G. (2017). Homes shortage and city prices based on student housing boom. *The Times*, Feburary 2.

Bickerton, C. (2016). *The European Union: A citizen's guide*. London: Penguin.

Blair, T. (1996). *Speech to the Labour Party Conference*, October 1. Blackpool.

Bok, D. (2003). *Universities in the Marketplace: The commercialization of American higher education*. Princeton, NJ: Princeton University Press.

Bourdieu, P. (1988). *Homo Academicus*. Palo Alto, CA: Stanford University Press.

Bourdieu, P. (2002). The forms of capital. In N. W. Biggart (Ed.), *Readings in economic sociology*. Oxford: Blackwell.

British Council. (2017). *Erasmus+ staff mobility*. Retrieved from https://www.britishcouncil.org/study-work-create/opportunity/work-volunteer/erasmus-staff-mobility

Brown, R. (2015). Education beyond the Gove Legacy: The case of higher education. In M. Finn, *The Gove Legacy: Education in Britain after the coalition*. London: Palgrave.

Brown, R., & Carasso, H. (2013). *Everything for sale? The marketization of UK higher education*. London: Routledge.

Burns, J. (2017). Universities run cartel, says think tank. *BBC News*, September. Retrieved from http://www.bbc.co.uk/news/education-41125111

Butler, P. (2013). Austerity: 'Unprecedented erosion' in living standards. *The Guardian* [online], June 28. Retrieved from https://www.theguardian.com/society/patrick-butler-cuts-blog/2013/jun/28/austerity-unprecedented-erosion-living-standards-poverty

Cannadine, D. (1998). *Class in Britain*. New Haven, CT: Yale University Press.

Cebrián, D. B. (2017). The great Brexit brain drain. *El País*, July 24. Retrieved from https://elpais.com/elpais/2017/07/19/inenglish/1500483801_779025.html

Clarke, H., Goodwin, M., & Whiteley, P. (2017). *Brexit: Why Britain voted to leave the European Union*. Cambridge: Cambridge University Press.

Coates, S. (2017). Leak reveals low-priority industries for Brexit talks. *The Times*, Feburary 10.

Cocozza, P. (2017). The party's over: How tuition fees ruined university life. *The Guardian*, July 11.

Collini, S. (1991). *Public moralists: Political thought and intellectual life in Britan, 1850-1939*. Oxford: Clarendon Press.

Collini, S. (2012). *What are universities for?* London: Penguin.

Collini, S. (2017). *Speaking of universities*. London: Verso.

Committee on Higher Education. (1963). *Higher education: Report of the committee*. London: HMSO.

Connelly, T. (2016). University of Liverpool EU law lecturer's incredible out-of-office email response in wake of Brexit abuse. *Legal Cheeck*, June 28. Retrieved from https://www.legalcheek.com/2016/06/university-of-liverpool-eu-law-lecturers-incredible-out-of-office-email-response-to-bremain-haters/

Conservative Party. (2015). *The Conservative Party manifesto*. Conservative Party.

Cook, C. (2015). *Home Secretary proposes tougher rules for student visas*. BBC News, July 16. Retrieved from http://www.bbc.co.uk/news/uk-politics-33561040

Corbett, A. (2016). *Higher education and research: Report of the hearing held on December 8, 2015*. LSE Commission on the Future of Britain in Europe. London: LSE.

Coughlan, S. (2015). University bosses earning £260,000. *BBC News*, March 4. Retrieved from http://www.bbc.co.uk/news/education-31715020

Coventry Observer. (2016). University Vice Chancellor calls on government to delay Higher Education Bill. *Coventry*

Observer, June 27. Retrieved from https://coventryobserver.
co.uk/news/university-vice-chancellor-calls-government-delay-
higher-education-bill/

CRASSH (Director). (2017). *Cambridge and the ERC:
Celebrating research excellence* [Motion Picture]. Retrieved
from http://www.crassh.cam.ac.uk/gallery/video/crassh-and-
the-erc-celebrating-research-excellence

Croft, S. (2017) (M. Finn, Interviewer), July 24. Interview.

Crosland, A. (1965, April 27). Speech at Woolwich
Polytechnic. Retrieved from http://www.hepi.ac.uk/wp-
content/uploads/2016/08/Scan-158.pdf

Cummings, B. (2016). *Written evidence to the House of
Commons Education Committee inquiry*, November.

Curtis, P. (2004). Language barrier turning students off
Europe. *The Guardian*, August 6. Retrieved from https://
www.theguardian.com/education/2004/aug/06/internationale-
ducationnews.highereducation

Dahlgreen, W. (2016). *The British Empire is 'something to
be proud of'*. YouGov, July 24. Retrieved from https://you-
gov.co.uk/news/2014/07/26/britain-proud-its-empire/

d'Ancona, M. (2017). *Post-Truth: The new war on truth and
how to fight back*. London: Ebury Press.

Dathan, M. (2017). EU thieving students. *The Sun*, March 2.

Davidson, R. (2017). British universities in the Brexit
moment (M. Finn, Interviewer), August 16.

Davies, J. (2016). *Written evidence to House of Commons
Education Committee inquiry*, September.

Davies, W. (2017). *The limits of neoliberalism: Authority,
sovereignty and the logic of competition*. London: SAGE.

Davis, E. (2017). *Post-Truth: Why we have reached peak bullshit and what we can do about it*. London: Little, Brown.

Deo, M. E. (2015). A bitter tenure battle: Fighting bias in teaching evaluations. *Columbia Journal of Gender and Law*.

Department for Business, Energy and Industrial Strategy. (2017a). *Horizon 2020 UK participation statistics: UK totals as of February 28th 2017*. London: Department of Business, Energy and Industrial Strategy.

Department for Business, Energy and Industrial Strategy. (2017b, February 20). *Terms of reference: High level stakeholder working group on EU exit, universities, research and innovation*. Retrieved from Department for Business, Energy and Industrial Strategy.

Department for Business, Energy and Industrial Strategy. (2017c). *UK strategy for the global challenges research fund*. London: TSO.

Department for Business, Energy and Industrial Strategy. (2017d). *Building our industrial strategy*. London: TSO.

Department for Business, Innovation and Skills. (2014). *Our plan for growth: Science and innovation*. London: TSO.

Department for Business, Innovation and Skills. (2016a). *Case for the creation of UK research and innovation*. London: TSO.

Department for Business, Innovation and Skills. (2016b). *Success as a knowledge economy: Teaching excellence, social mobility and student choice*. London: The Stationery Office.

Department for Education. (2016). *Participation rates in higher education: Academic years 2006/2007 - 2014/2015 (provisional)*. London: Department for Education.

Dickinson, J. (2017). The OfS should make university governance a top priority. *WonkHE*, August 31. Retrieved from http://wonkhe.com/blogs/the-ofs-should-make-university-governance-a-top-priority/

Dnes, A. W., & Seaton, J. S. (1998). The reform of academic tenure in the United Kingdom. *International Review of Law and Economics*, *18*, 491–509.

Dorey, P. (2015). 'Well, Harold insists on having it!' — The political struggle to establish the open university, 1965–67. *Contemporary British History*, *29*(2).

Dougan, M. (2017a). Editor's introduction. In M. Dougan (Ed.), *The UK after Brexit: Legal and policy challenges*. Cambridge: Intersentia.

Dougan, M. (2017b). British universities in the Brexit moment (M. Finn, Interviewer), August 21.

d'Urso, J. (2017). Does it matter if the UK leaves Euratom? *BBC News*, July 12. Retrieved from http://www.bbc.co.uk/news/uk-politics-uk-leaves-the-eu-40571853

Eaton, G. (2017). The Grenfell Tower fire has turned a spotlight on austerity's limits. *New Statesman*, June 15. Retrieved from http://www.newstatesman.com/politics/uk/2017/06/grenfell-tower-fire-has-turned-spotlight-austeritys-limits

Economist, T. (2017). Hungary passes a law to shut down a bothersome university. *Economist*, April 8.

Edge Hill University. (2016). *Written evidence to the House of Commons Education Committee inquiry*.

Edgerton, D. (2005). *Warfare state: Britain, 1920-1970*. Cambridge: Cambridge University Press.

Edwards, L. (2016). Brexit: You don't know what you've got till it's gone. *ScriptEd*, *13*(2).

Ellis, H., & Kircheberger, U. (2014). *Anglo-German scholarly networks in the long nineteenth century*. Leiden: Brill.

Else, H. (2017a). Brexit department lacks scientific adviser as talks get under way. *Times Higher Education*, July 18. Retrieved from https://www.timeshighereducation.com/news/brexit-department-lacks-scientific-adviser-as-talks-get-under-way

Else, H. (2017b). Decision to leave Euratom 'bonkers', say experts. *Times Higher Education*, January 27. Retrieved from https://www.timeshighereducation.com/news/decision-leave-euratom-bonkers-say-experts

Enders, J. (1998). Academic staff mobility in the European Community: The ERASMUS experience. *Comparative Education Review*, *42*(1).

Engineering and Technology. (2016). *UK to lose billions in EU research funding after Brexit*. E&T, December 9. Retrieved from https://eandt.theiet.org/content/articles/2016/12/uk-to-lose-billions-in-eu-research-funding-after-brexit/

European Commission. (2003). *The role of universities in the Europe of knowledge*. Brussels: European Commission. Retrieved from http://eur-lex.europa.eu/legal-content/EN/TXT/?uri=LEGISSUM:c11067

European Commission. (2014a). *Erasmus+ — Facts, figures and trends*. Brussels: European Commission.

European Commission. (2014b). *Horizon 2020 in brief: The European framework programme for research and innovation*. Brussels: European Commission.

European Commission. (2016). *Eramus+ programme guide, 2016-17*. Brussels: European Commission.

European Commission. (2017a). *European citizenship*. European Commission, August 28. Retrieved from http://ec.europa.eu/justice/citizen/

European Commission. (2017b). *Marie Curie-Sklodowska actions*. European Commission, September 1. Retrieved from https://ec.europa.eu/programmes/horizon2020/en/h2020-section/marie-sklodowska-curie-actions

European Union. (2012). *Eramsus: Changing lives, opening minds for 25 years*. Brussels: European Union.

Financial Times. (2017). Archaeology and Classics threatend by research cuts after Brexit. *Financial Times*, May 24.

Finn, M. (2002). The new elite. *The Guardian*, November 27. Retrieved from https://www.theguardian.com/education/2002/nov/27/highereducation.uk1

Finn, M. (2015a). *The Gove Legacy: Education in Britain after the coalition*. London: Palgrave.

Finn, M. (2015b). The coming of the coalition and the coalition agreement. In A. Seldon & M. Finn, *The coalition effect, 2010-2015*. Cambridge: Cambridge University Press.

Finn, M. (2015c). Education beyond the Gove Legacy: The case of higher education (2) — Ideology in action. In M. Finn (Ed.), *The Gove Legacy: Education in Britain after the coalition*. London: Palgrave.

Finn, M. (2016a). 'Insularity is not the way forward: Three university vice-chancellors on Brexit. *The Conversation*, June 13. Retrieved from https://theconversation.com/insularity-is-not-the-way-forward-three-university-vice-chancellors-on-brexit-60660

Finn, M. (2016b). Post-war fantasies and Brexit: The delusional view of Britain's place in the world. *LSE Politics and Policy*, June 21. Retrieved from http://eprints.lse.ac.uk/71421/1/blogs.lse.ac.uk-Post-war%20fantasies%20and%20Brexit%20the%20delusional%20view%20of%20Britains%20place%20in%20the%20world.pdf

Finn, M. (2016c). Paradigm shift. *Political Insight*, 7(3).

Finn, M. (2018a). *Socialism, education and equal opportunity: The contemporary legacy of Anthony Crosland*. London: Palgrave.

Finn, M. (2018b). The never-ending crisis in British higher education. In T. Geelan, P. Walsh, & M. Gonzalez-Hernando (Eds.), *From financial crisis to social change: Towards alternative horizons*. London: Palgrave.

Finn, M. (2019). *Empire state: British political culture in the age of neonationalism*. London: Routledge.

Finn, M., & Seldon, A. (2013). Constitutional reform since 1997: The historians' perspective. In M. Qvortrup (Ed.), *The British Constitution: Continuity and change*. Oxford: Hart.

Finn, M. T. (2012). The political economy of higher education in England, c. 1944-1974. Unpublished Cambridge PhD dissertation, University of Cambridge, Cambridge.

Fisher, M. (2009). *Capitalist realism: Is there no alternative?* London: Zero Books.

Fisher, S., Hanretty, C., & Jennings, W. (2017). *Expert predictions of the 2017 UK General Election*. London: Political Studies Association.

Flinders, M. (2009). *Democratic drift: Majoritarian modifica-tion and democratic anomie in the United Kingdom*. Oxford: Oxford University Press.

Ford, R., & Goodwin, M. (2014). *Revolt on the Right: Explaining support for the radical right in Britain*. London: Routledge.

Fort, A. (2003). *Prof: The life and times of Frederick Lindemann*. London: Pimlico.

Fox, C. (2016). *I find that offensive*. London: Biteback.

Franco-Santos, M., & Otley, D. (2017). The Tef won't improve teaching — Universities will just play the game. *The Guardian*, June 22. Retrieved from https://www.theguardian.com/higher-education-network/2017/jun/22/the-tef-wont-improve-teaching-universities-will-just-play-the-game

Freeman, M. (2015). EU science funding: 'The UK cannot afford to lose out on this pot of money'. *The Guardian*, May 13. Retrieved from https://www.theguardian.com/higher-education-network/2015/may/13/eu-science-funding-the-uk-cannot-afford-to-lose-out-on-this-pot-of-money

Furedi, F. (2010). Introduction. In M. Molesworth, R. Scullion, & E. Nixon (Eds.), *The marketisation of higher education and the student as consumer*. London: Routledge.

Gardiner, L. (2016). *Stagnation generation: The case for reneweing the intergenerational contract*. London: Resolution Foundation. Retrieved from http://www.intergencommission.org/wp-content/uploads/2016/07/Intergenerational-commis-sion-launch-report.pdf

Garner, R. (2014). The academic fat cats: Vice-chancellors at Britain's top universities get £22,000 pay rises — As lecturers are stuck on 1 per cent. *The Independent*, January 2.

Retrieved from http://www.independent.co.uk/student/news/
university-chiefs-under-fire-for-huge-pay-rises-after-tuition-
fee-hikes-9034893.html

Gibbs, A. (2014). UK students trailing peers on take-up of
Erasmus exchanges. *The Conversation*, May 22. Retrieved
from https://theconversation.com/uk-students-trailing-eu-
peers-on-take-up-of-erasmus-exchanges-26783

Gilligan, A. (2017). Universities take foreign students ahead
of British. *Sunday Times*, August 6.

Giroux, H. A. (2014). *Neoliberalism's war on higher education*. Chicago: Haymarket Books.

Goldhill, S. (2017). British universities in the Brexit moment
(M. Finn, Interviewer), August 22.

Goodhart, D. (2017). *The road to somewhere: The populist
revolt and the future of politics*. London: Hurst.

Gove, M. (2013, September 5). *The importance of teaching:
Speech to policy exchange*. London: Gov.uk.

Gove, M. (2017). Mrs May is our first Catholic Prime
Minister. *The Times*, March 9.

Grant, M. (2016a). 'Citizen of the world?' Think again.
British citizenship after Brexit. *Democratic Audit*, November
21. Retrieved from http://www.democraticaudit.com/2016/
11/21/citizen-of-the-world-think-again-british-citizenship-
after-brexit/

Grant, M. (2016b). Historicizing citizenship in post-war
Britain. *Historical Journal*, *59*(4).

Graphene Research Centre. (2017, September 1). *What can
graphene do?* Retrieved from http://www.graphene.manche-
ster.ac.uk/explore/what-can-graphene-do/

Green, C. (2014). EU's Eramsus study abroad programme is responsible for 1m babies'. *The Independent*, September 23.

Green, J. (2016). *Written evidence to House of Commons Education Committee inquiry*, October.

Grove, J. (2013). Horizon 2020 and Erasmus budgets approved. *Times Higher Education*, November 21. Retrieved from https://www.timeshighereducation.com/news/horizon-2020-and-erasmus-budgets-approved/2009234.article

Grove, J. (2016). HE Bill second reading: 'post-Brexit vote pause needed', say critics. *Times Higher Education*, July 19. Retrieved from https://www.timeshighereducation.com/news/he-bill-second-reading-post-brexit-vote-pause-needed-say-critics

The Guardian. (2016a). Letters: The higher education bill will harm universities. *The Guardian*, September 29.

The Guardian. (2016b). *The Guardian* view on universities: Facing a double whammy. *The Guardian*, September 22. Retrieved from https://www.theguardian.com/commentisfree/2016/sep/22/the-guardian-view-on-universities-facing-a-double-whammy

The Guardian. (2017). Mental health: A university crisis. *The Guardian*, September 7. Retrieved from https://www.theguardian.com/education/series/mental-health-a-university-crisis

Harvey, D. (2005). *A brief history of neoliberalism*. Oxford: Oxford University Press.

Hastings, A., Bailey, N., Besemer, K., Bramley, G., Gannon, M., & Watkins, D. (2013). *Coping with the cuts? Local*

government and poorer communities. York: Joseph
Rowntree Foundation.

Havergal, C. (2016). Three-quarters of students 'angry about
Brexit'. *Times Higher Education*, July. Retrieved from https://
www.timeshighereducation.com/news/three-quarters-stu-
dents-angry-about-brexit

Hayes, D. (2016). After Brexit, snowflake professors need to
grow up. *Spiked!*, December 12. Retrieved from http://www.
spiked-online.com/newsite/article/after-brexit-snowflake-
professor-need-to-grow-up/19087#.WaNBdiiGO00

HEFCE. (2017, September). Initial decisions on the Research
Excellence Framework 2021. Retrieved from http://www.
hefce.ac.uk/media/HEFCE,2014/Content/Pubs/
Independentresearch/2017/REF,201701/REF2017_01.pdf

Hegan, B. (2016). *Written evidence to the House of
Commons Education Committee Inquiry*, October.

Hennessy, P. (1989). *Whitehall*. London: Pimlico.

HEPI. (2015a). *Now that's what we call 'soft power': 55
world leaders educated in the UK*. HEPI, October 1.
Retrieved from http://www.hepi.ac.uk/2015/10/01/now-thats-
call-soft-power-55-world-leaders-educated-uk/

HEPI. (2015b). *World leaders who have studied in the UK*.
HEPI, September 22. Retrieved from http://www.hepi.ac.uk/
wp-content/uploads/2015/10/World-leaders-who-have-
studied-in-the-UK-22-Sept-2015.xlsx

HEPI. (2015c). *New HEPI/Kaplan research shows benefits of
studying alongside international students*. HEPI, March 19.
Retrieved from http://www.hepi.ac.uk/2015/03/19/new-
hepikaplan-research-shows-benefits-studying-alongside-
international-students/

HEPI. (2017). *Reality check: A report on university applicants' attitudes and perceptions.* Oxford: HEPI.

Higher Education Funding Council for England. (2017).
The teaching excellence framework. *HEFCE*, September 3.
Retrieved from: http://www.hefce.ac.uk/lt/tef/

Hillman, N. (2016). The coalition's higher education reforms
in England. *Oxford Review of Education, 42*(3).

Hinson, S. (2017). *Euratom.* London: House of Commons
Library.

House of Commons Business, Energy and Industrial Strategy
Committee. (2017). *Leaving the EU: Negotiating priorities
for energy and climate change policy.* London: House of
Commons.

House of Commons Education Committee. (2017). *Exiting
the EU: Challenges and opportunities for higher education.*
London: House of Commons.

House of Lords Science and Technology Commitee. (2016).
EU membership and UK science. London: House of Lords.

Howker, E., & Malik, S. (2010). *The Jilted generation: How
Britain has bankrupted its youth.* London: Icon Books.

Hubble, S. (2016). *The impact of leaving the EU on higher
education.* London: House of Commons Library.

Hughes, A. (2011). Open innovation, the Haldane principle
and the new production of knowledge: science policy and
university–industry links in the UK after the financial crisis.
Prometheus.

Huitson, L. (2016). *Written evidence submitted to House of
Commons Education Committee Inquiry,* November.

Husbands, C. (2016). British universities and Brexit (M. Finn, Interviewer), June.

Husbands, C. (2017). TEF results — The chair's post-match analysis. *WonkHE*, June 23. Retrieved from http://wonkhe.com/blogs/tef-results-the-chairs-post-match-analysis/

Ibrahim, J. (2014). The moral economy of the student protest movement 2010-2011. *Contemporary Social Science*, 9(1).

Jackson, B. (2010). At the origins of neo-liberalism: The free economy and the strong state, 1930-1947. *Historical Journal*, 53(1).

James, C. (2016). Brexit: What now for study mobility between Britain and the EU? *Pécs Journal of European and International Law, II*.

Johnson, J. (2016a). *Speech to Universities UK annual conference, Nottingham*. gov.uk, September 7. Retrieved from https://www.gov.uk/government/speeches/jo-johnson-universities-uk-annual-conference-2016

Johnson, J. (2016b). Universities must wipe out mediocre teaching and drive up student engagement. *Daily Telegraph*, August 17.

Johnston, I. (2016). Racist, xenophobic and anti-intellectual: Academics threaten to leave Brexit Britain. *The Independent*, July 12.

Jones, A. (2014). Elite science and the BBC: A 1950s contest of ownership. *BJHS*, 47(4).

Kaufmann, E. (2016). Brexit voters: NOT the 'left behind'. *Fabian Review*, June 24. Retrieved from http://www.fabians.org.uk/brexit-voters-not-the-left-behind/

Kaur, K. (2017, April 13). *What the British public really think about international students*. Retrieved from http://www.universitiesuk.ac.uk/blog/Pages/What-the-British-public-really-think-about-international-students.aspx

Kershaw, A. (2011). Cambridge ranked as best university in the world. *The Independent*, September 4.

Kettle, M. (2016). David Cameron gambled and lost. He had to go. *The Guardian*, September 12.

Knapton, S. (2017). Universities to be stopped from sidelining British students for foreign teens who can pay more. *Daily Telegraph*, August 6. Retrieved from http://www.telegraph.co.uk/education/2017/08/06/universities-stopped-sidelining-british-students-foreign-teens/

Labour Party. (1997). *New labour: Because Britain deserves better*. London: Labour Party.

Lawrence, J. (2000). The British sense of class. *Journal of Contemporary History*, *35*(2).

Leavis, F. R. (2013 [1962]). *Two cultures? The significance of C. P. Snow*. Cambridge: Cambridge University Press.

Lybeck, E. R. (2017). Academics need a guild of their own. *Times Higher Education*, September 4. Retrieved from https://www.timeshighereducation.com/blog/academics-need-guild-their-own

Lybeck, E. R. (2018). The coming crisis of academic authority. In T. Geelan, P. Walsh, & M. Gonzalez-Hernando (Eds.), *From financial crisis to social change: Towards alternative horizons*. London: Palgrave.

Macilwain, C. (2017, January 5). Scientists should not resign themselves to Brexit. *Nature*, *541*.

Maidment, J. (2017). Theresa May commits Tories to cutting net migration to the UK to the tens of thousands. *Daily Telegraph*, April 20. Retrieved from http://www.telegraph.co.uk/news/2017/04/20/theresa-may-commits-tories-cutting-net-migration-uk-tens-thousands/

Mance, H. (2016). Britain has had enough of experts, says Gove. *Financial Times*, June 3.

Mandelson, P., & Liddle, R. (1996). *The Blair revolution: Can new labour deliver?* London: Faber and Faber.

Mandler, P. (2016). Britain's EU problem is a London problem. *Dissent*, June 24.

Marginson, S. (2017a). Higher education and research are the 'collateral damage' of Brexit. *Times Higher Education*, September 13. Retrieved from https://www.timeshighereducation.com/blog/higher-education-and-research-are-collateral-damage-brexit

Marginson, S. (2017b). Universities: 'The collateral damage of blood and soil nationalist politics'. *Times Higher Education*, March 5. Retrieved from https://www.timeshighereducation.com/opinion/universities-collateral-damage-blood-and-soil-nationalist-politics

Mayhew, K. (2016). UK higher education and Brexit. *Oxford Review of Economic Policy*, *33*(S1).

McCormac, G. (2016). British universities and Brexit (M. Finn, Interviewer), June 6.

McIvor, J. (2017). Uncertainty over EU students in Scotland after Brexit. *BBCNews*, March 27. Retrieved from: http://www.bbc.co.uk/news/uk-scotland-scotland-politics-39408057

Mckenzie, L. (2017a). 'It's not ideal': Reconsidering 'anger' and 'apathy' in the Brexit vote among an invisible working class. *Competition & Change*, *21*(3).

Mckenzie, L. (2017b). The middle-class academic elite is totally out of touch. *Times Higher Education*, September 2.

Merrick, R. (2017). Theresa May's deputy accused of misleading MPs after insisting cancer patients have nothing to fear from UK leaving Euratom. *The Independent*, July 12. Retrieved from http://www.independent.co.uk/news/uk/politics/theresa-may-damien-greene-nhs-cancer-patients-brexit-uk-quit-euratom-eu-agency-mps-european-union-a7837356.html

Ministry of Education. (1956). *Technical education*. London: HMSO.

Moore-Bridger, B. (2017). Leading Finnish historian threatened with detention and deportation in "absurd" Brexit ruling by Home Office officials. *Evening Standard*, August 23. Retrieved from https://www.standard.co.uk/news/uk/leading-finnish-historian-threatened-with-detention-and-deportation-in-absurd-brexit-ruling-by-home-a3618176.html

Morgan, J. (2016). EU referendum: Nine out of 10 university staff back Remain. *Times Higher Education*, June 16. Retrieved from https://www.timeshighereducation.com/news/european-union-referendum-nine-out-of-ten-university-staff-back-remain

Morgan, J. (2017a). EU student applications to UK down 7% after Brexit vote. *Times Higher Education*, February 2. Retrieved from https://www.timeshighereducation.com/news/eu-student-applications-uk-down-7-per-cent-after-brexit-vote

Morgan, J. (2017b). Forging a new alloy. *Times Higher Education*, August 10.

Morland, S. (2017). Academics challenge Warwick University over workers' rights reform. *The Boar*, April 6. Retrieved from https://theboar.org/2017/04/ucu-challenges-university-workers-rights-reform/

Morris, D. (2017a). What *The Sunday Times* got wrong on 'crowding out' British students. *WonkHE*, August 8. Retrieved from http://wonkhe.com/blogs/what-the-sunday-times-got-wrong-on-crowding-out-british-students/

Morris, D. (2017b). Be it enacted: The Higher Education and Research Act. *WonkHE*, April 27. Retrieved from http://wonkhe.com/blogs/be-it-enacted-the-higher-education-and-research-act-2017/

Morris, D. (2017c). Why don't they like us? A terrible two months for universities in the news. *WonkHE*, July 31. Retrieved from http://wonkhe.com/blogs/why-dont-they-like-us-a-terrible-two-months-for-universities-in-the-news/

Morris, J. (2016). *The 15 things you need to know about Remain voters*. London: New Economics Foundation.

Murphy, E. (2017). Stop celebrating the TEF results — Your hypocrisy is galling! *Times Higher Education*, June 23. Retrieved from https://www.timeshighereducation.com/blog/stop-celebrating-tef-results-your-hypocrisy-galling

Murray, S. K. (1957). Foreword. In U. G. Committee (Ed.), *Report of the sub-committee on university residence*. London: HMSO.

N8 Regional Partnership. (2016). *The Power of 8: Knowledge, innovation and growth for the north*. Manchester: N8Regional Partnership.

Niemietz, K. (2016). *The UK health system: An international comparison of health outcomes*. London: UK2020.

Nurse, P. (2015). *Ensuring a successful UK research endeavour: A review of the UK research councils*. London: Department of Business, Innovation and Skills.

Office for National Statistics. (2013). *Graduates in the UK labour market*. London: ONS.

Oliver, C. (2016). *Unleashing demons: The inside story of Brexit*. London: Hodder & Stoughton.

O'Neill, O. (2002). *A question of trust: The BBC Reith Lectures 2002*. Cambridge: Cambridge University Press.

Ortolano, G. (2009). *The two cultures controversy: Science, literature and cultural politics in postwar Britain*. Cambridge: Cambridge University Press.

Osborne, R. (2017). British univerisites in the Brexit moment (M. Finn, Interviewer), August 21.

Osler, A. (1998). European citizenship and study abroad: Student teachers experiences and identities. *Cambridge Journal of Education, 28*(1).

Papatsiba, V. (2005). Political and individual rationales of student mobility: A case study of ERAMUS and a French regional scheme for studies abroad. *European Journal of Education, 40*(2), 173–188.

Parkin, S. (2017). Brexit: Scientist behind one of the century's most important discoveries set to leave UK over EU exit. *The Independent*, August 10. Retrieved from http://www.independent.co.uk/news/science/brexit-latest-scientist-andre-geim-graphene-discovery-university-manchester-eu-exit-with-drawal-a7886416.html

Parr, C. (2017). Andrew Adonis hits out at academics
(and academics hit back). *Times Higher Education*, July 13.
Retrieved from https://www.timeshighereducation.com/
blog/andrew-adonis-hits-out-academics-and-academics-hit-
back

Peal, R. (2014). *Progressively worse: The burden of bad ideas
in British schools*. London: Civitas.

Phillips, D. (1980). Lindsay and the German universities: An
Oxford contribution to the post-war reform debate. *Oxford
Review of Education*, 6(1).

Polanyi, M. (1962). The republic of science: Its political and
economic theory. *Minerva*, *1*(1).

Popper, K. (2002 [1959]). *The logic of scientific discovery*.
London: Routledge.

Press Association. (2016). Oxford becomes first UK university to top global rankings. *The Guardian*, September 22.

Ramirez, A. (2015). This is the 'miracle material' that will
change everything. *TIME*, July 20. Retrieved from http://
time.com/3964302/miracle-material-graphene-graphite/

Rayner, G., & Hope, C. (2017). Cut the EU red tape choking
Britain after Brexit to set the country free from the shackles
of Brussels. *Daily Telegraph*, March 28. Retrieved from
http://www.telegraph.co.uk/news/2017/03/27/cut-eu-red-
tape-choking-britain-brexit-set-country-free-shackles/

Research Councils UK. (2014). *Impact acceleration
accounts — A common Research Councils approach*.
Research Councils UK. Retrieved from http://www.rcuk.ac.
uk/innovation/impact-accelerator-accounts/

de Ridder-Symoens, H. (1992). *A history of the university in Europe: Volume 1, Universities in the middle ages.* Cambridge: Cambridge University Press.

Robbins, L. (1966a). Expansion and the binary system. In L. Robbins (Ed.), *The university in the modern world.* London: Macmillan.

Robbins, L. (1966b). The university in the modern World. In L. Robbins (Ed.), *The University in the modern world.* London: Macmillan.

Roberts, R. (2017). Jeremy Corbyn accused of breaking a promise he never made on student debt. *The Independent*, July 23. Retrieved from http://www.independent.co.uk/news/uk/politics/jeremy-corbyn-labour-student-loans-debt-manifesto-pledge-amnesty-cancel-tuition-fees-a7856161.html

Rohn, J., Curry, S., & Steele, A. (2015). UK research funding slumps below 0.5% GDP – Putting us last in the G8. *The Guardian*, March 13. Retrieved from https://www.theguardian.com/science/occams-corner/2015/mar/13/science-vital-uk-spending-research-gdp

Rothschild, E. (1999). Globalisation and the return of history. *Foreign Policy.*

Royal Society. (2015). *UK research and the European Union: The role of the EU in funding UK research.* London: Royal Society.

Rudd, A. (2016). *Speech to the Conservative Party Conference*, October 4. Manchester.

Runciman, D. (2016a). A win for 'proper people?': Brexit as a rejection of the networked world. *Juncture*, *23*(1).

Runciman, D. (2016b). How the education gap is tearing politics apart. *The Guardian*, October 5.

Russell Group. (2016). *Response to House of Commons Education Committee enquiry*. London: Russell Group.

Russell Group. (2017, February). Russell Group universities and Brexit. Retrieved from https://www.russellgroup.ac.uk/media/5468/russell-group-universities-and-brexit-briefing-note-february-2017.pdf

Sanderson, M. (1991). Social equity and industrial need: A dilemma of English education since 1945. In T. R. Gourvish & A. O'Day (Eds.), *Britain since 1945*. London: Macmillan.

Sanderson, M. (2002). *The history of the University of East Anglia, Norwich*. London: Hambledon Continuum.

Savage, M. (2016). Got a job offer from a continental European university just now. That was quick! *Twitter*, June 24. Retrieved from https://twitter.com/MikeSav47032563/status/746263548775534592

Savage, M. (2017). Fear of Brexit brain drain as EU nationals leave British universities. *Observer*, June 4.

Sayer, D. (2017). White riot—Brexit, Trump, and post-factual politics. *Historical Sociology*, *30*.

Scientists for EU. (2017). *Scientists for EU*. Retrieved from http://www.scientistsforeu.uk/. Accessed on August 28, 2017.

Scott Crines, A. (2016). *Referendum analysis*. Retrieved from http://www.referendumanalysis.eu/eu-referendum-analysis-2016/section-5-campaign-and-political-communication/the-rhetoric-of-the-eu-referendum-campaign/

Seldon, A. (2015). Students don't deserve this rotten deal. *The Times*, November 7.

Seldon, A. (2017). Foreword. In R. Tice, & T. Al-Humaidi (Eds.), *Timebomb: How the university cartel is failing Britain's students*. London: UK 2020.

Sellgren, K. (2016). University bosses' pay 'inflation-busting'. *BBC News*, Feburary 11. Retrieved from http://www.bbc.co.uk/news/education-35541780

Shattock, M. (2012). *Making policy in British higher education, 1945-2011*. Maidenhead: Open University Press.

Shipman, T. (2016). *All-out war: The full story of how Brexit sunk Britain's political class*. London: William Collins.

Smith, J. (2015). The coalition and Europe: The coalition's poisoned chalice. In A. Seldon & M. Finn (Eds.), *The coalition effect, 2010-2015*. Cambridge: Cambridge University Press.

Smith, J. (2017). *The UK's journeys into and out of the EU: Destinations unknown*. Abingdon: Routledge.

Smyth, J. (2017). *The Toxic University: Zombie leadership, academic rock stars, and neoliberal ideology*. London: Palgrave.

Snell, D. (2017). Jeez you guys seem caught in privileged middle class thinking. Back in the real world where you don't have money IT needs to work. *Twitter*, August 17. Retrieved from https://twitter.com/DanielSnellAE/status/898099071159848964

Snow, C. P. (1961). *The two cultures and the scientific revolution*. Cambridge: Cambridge University Press.

Sparrow, A. (2017). Former Theresa May aide attacks tuition fees 'Ponzi scheme'. *The Guardian*, August 17. Retrieved from https://www.theguardian.com/education/2017/aug/17/

former-theresa-may-aide-attacks-tuition-fees-ponzi-scheme-nick-timothy

Stedman Jones, D. (2012). *Masters of the Universe: Hayek, Friedman and the birth of neoliberal politics*. Princeton, NJ: Princeton University Press.

Stevens, R. (2004). *University to Uni: The politics of higher education since 1944*. London: Politico's.

Stewart, H. (2017). Exit checks data raises questions over May's focus on student overstayers. *The Guardian*, August 24.

Stewart, H., Mason, R., & Grierson, J. (2017). Theresa May under fire as student visa myth exposed. *The Guardian*, August 24.

Stocker, P. (2017). *English uprising: Brexit and the mainstreaming of the far right*. London: Melville House.

Suiter, J. (2016). Post-truth politics. *Political Insight*, 7(3).

Sutcliffe-Braithwaite, F. (2012). Neo-liberalism and morality in the making of Thatcherite social policy. *Historical Journal*, 55(2).

Talbot, C. (2017). No longer welcome: The EU academics in Britain told to 'make arrangements to leave'. *LSE EUROPP*, January 27.

Technopolis. (2017). *The role of EU funding in UK research and innovation*. London: Technopolis. Retrieved from https://royalsociety.org/~/media/policy/Publications/2017/2017-05-technopolis-role-of-EU-funding-report.PDF

Thompson, M. (2016). *Enough said: What's gone wrong with the language of politics?* London: Bodley Head.

Tice, R., & Al-Humaidhi, T. (2017). *Timebomb: How the university cartel is failing Britain's students*. London: UK2020.

Times Higher Education. (2017). Teaching excellence framework (TEF) results 2017. *Times Higher Education*, June 22. Retrieved from https://www.timeshighereducation.com/news/teaching-excellence-framework-tef-results-2017

Tonkin, B. (2016). Too much 'balance' can undermine fair debate and democracy. *The Independent*, March 11.

Tooley, J. (2001). *Buckingham at 25*. London: Institute of Economic Affairs.

Trentmann, F. (1998). Political culture and political economy: Interest, ideology and free trade. *Review of International Political Economy*, *5*(2).

Trinity College, Cambridge. (2017). *Trinity's senior tutor on the consequences of a 'hard Brexit' for UK universities*. Trinity College, Cambridge, January 12: Retrieved from https://www.trin.cam.ac.uk/news/trinitys-senior-tutor-warns-of-consequences-of-a-hard-brexit-for-uk-universities/

Truscot, B. (1944). *Redbrick University*. London: Faber and Faber.

UK Erasmus+ National Agency. (2016). *Written evidence submitted by the UK Erasmus+ National Agency*, November.

UKRI. (2017). *UK research and innovation*. Retrieved from http://www.ukri.org/. Accessed on August 28, 2017.

Universities UK. (2015). *Patterns and trends in UK higher education 2015*. London: Universities UK.

Universities UK. (2016a). *Effect of exiting the EU on higher education*. London: Universities UK.

Universities UK. (2016b, April 8). *EU students vital to regional economies and jobs*. Retrieved from http://www.universitiesuk.ac.uk/news/Pages/eu-students-vital-to-regional-economies.aspx

Universities UK. (2016c). *Written evidence to House of Commons Education Committee inquiry*. London: Universities UK.

Universities UK. (2017). *Patterns and trends in higher education 2017*. London: Universities UK.

University Grants Committee. (1957). *Report of the sub-committee on halls of residence*. London: HMSO.

University of Sheffield. (2016, September 18). *Top northern universities' impact double that of Premier League*. Retrieved from https://www.sheffield.ac.uk/news/nr/northern-universities-n8-report-northern-powerhouse-brexit-premier-league-1.645147

Vasagar, J. (2010). University graduates should pay more for degrees, says minister. *The Guardian*, September 9. Retrieved from https://www.theguardian.com/education/2010/sep/09/david-willetts-graduate-tax-university

Vulliamy, E. (2016). Erasmus scheme may exclude British students after Brexit. *Observer*, July 24.

Walker, O., & Warrell, H. (2017). UK university applications down for first time since 2012. *The Guardian*, July 13. Retrieved from https://www.ft.com/content/cb91abe6-6792-11e7-8526-7b38dcaef614

Watt, N. (2014). Cameron edging UK towards EU exit with negotiation strategy, says Miliband. *The Guardian*, June 30.

Weale, S. (2016). UK university applications from EU down by 9%, says Ucas. *The Guardian*, October 27. Retrieved from https://www.theguardian.com/education/2016/oct/27/uk-university-applications-from-eu-down-9-ucas

Wellcome Trust. (2017). *Data protection regulation. Wellcome Trust*, September 3. Retrieved from https://wellcome.ac.uk/what-we-do/our-work/our-policy-work-data-protection-regulation

Wellings, B. (2016). Our Island Story: England, Europe and the Anglosphere alternative. *Political Studies Review*, *14*(3).

Wheeler, D. (2017). Shiny veneer, rotten within: A cancerous, consumer-drive capitalism has weakened higher education. *Times Higher Education*, August 10.

Whyte, W. (2015). *Redbrick: A social and architectural history of Britain's civic universities*. Oxford: Oxford University Press.

Wigram, M. (2016). *Switzerland and the Horizon 2020 programme*. Scientists for Britain, June 20. Retrieved from : http://scientistsforbritain.uk/wordpress/?p=271

Williams, M. (2016). *Written evidence to House of Commons Education Committee inquiry*, November.

Wilson, I. (2011). What should we expect of Erasmus generations? *Journal of Common Market Studies*, *49*(5), 1113–1140.

Winn, J. (2014). Co-operative higher education. *Reimaging the University: Keynote talk at the University of Gloucester*. Retrieved from http://josswinn.org/2014/10/18/reimagining-the-university/

Wolf, A. (2003). *Does education matter? Myths about education and economic growth*. Harmondsworth: Penguin.

Woodward, W., & Smithers, R. (2003). Clarke dismisses medieval historians. *The Guardian*, May 9. Retrieved from https://www.theguardian.com/uk/2003/may/09/highereducation.politics

Yeo, C. (2017). Britain's miserly post-Brexit offer to EU nationals shows a disdain for rights. *The Guardian*, July 6.

YouGov. (2016). *EU referendum debate: Trust fieldwork*. London: YouGov. Retrieved from https://d25d2506sfb94s.cloudfront.net/cumulus_uploads/document/x4iynd1mn7/TodayResults_160614_EUReferendum_W.pdf

Young, M. (1958). *The rise of the meritocracy*. Harmondswroth: Penguin.

INDEX